BIBLE RECORDS

OF

WASHINGTON COUNTY, MARYLAND

From Copies, Notes and in Some Cases,
the Bibles Themselves – on File at the
Washington County Historical Society

In Cooperation with the
Washington County Historical Society
Hagerstown, Maryland

F. Edward Wright

HERITAGE BOOKS
2020

HERITAGE BOOKS
AN IMPRINT OF HERITAGE BOOKS, INC.

Books, CDs, and more—Worldwide

For our listing of thousands of titles see our website
at
www.HeritageBooks.com

Published 2020 by
HERITAGE BOOKS, INC.
Publishing Division
5810 Ruatan Street
Berwyn Heights, Md. 20740

International Standard Book Number
Paperbound: 978-1-58549-235-0

INTRODUCTION

Among the many elusive sources of family history are family Bibles. One of the first objects of genealogical research, they oft times remain hidden or lost.

For those in search of Washington County families the quest may lead to the Washington County Historical Library. Here, under the domain of the librarian, Peggy Bledsoe, a number of Bibles are held, together with an even larger number of copies of family records and transcriptions taken from Bibles. A major portion of the records are handwritten transcriptions and notes done by Rachel S. Swartz. Ms. Swartz was a long-time volunteer of the Society. Her transcriptions and notes are contained in a notebook held by the Society.

The reader is cautioned that the data found in this publication represents, in large part, transcriptions of another transcription. One should attempt to evaluate each source and seek confirmation whenever possible.

A small part of the collection was omitted from this publication, namely those items which were copies of other published work.

Thanks to the Washington County Historical Society for their helpfulness and confidence in our efforts, and especially the efforts and patience of Peggy Bledsoe.

F. Edward Wright
Westminster, Maryland
1992

Bibles at Washington County Historical Society in which there are family records:

No. 2. Ridenour Family Bible

Jacob Ridenour b. March 8, 1828

Susannah Ridenour b. Oct 15, 1824

Mary Ellen Rebecca Ridenour b. Nov 11, 1850

John Henry Ridenour b. Jan 28, 1852

Nandy Catharine Ridenour b. Sep 27, 1853

George Melanchthon Ridenour b. Feb 25, 1855

Daniel Nuton Ridenour b. Dec 18, 1856

Charles Edward Ridenour b. Aug 28, 1858

Sarah Ann Elizabeth Ridenour b. Apr 3, 1860

Lewis Maclelon Ridenour b. Oct 5, 1861

Emma Arbelon Ridenour b. Feb 27, 18--

Daniel Newton Ridenour d. Sep 19, 1851, age 9 mos., 1 day.

Lewis Maclelon Ridenour d. Apr 27, 1862

Effa Jane Ridenour d. Aug 7, 1869

Laura Etta & Effa Jane Ridenour, both b. Sep 13, 1866

Susannah Ifert b. Oct 15, 1824

John Henry Ifert b. Sep 24 1826

William Ifert b. Oct 6, 1828

Daniel Ifert b. Feb 12, 1831

No. 3. Knox Family Bible

Samuel Knox m. Margaret Witherow, Mar 15, 1821

Rachel Rebecca Knox m. James H. Marsh Dec 5, 1842

Samuel Knox m. Mary E. Culbertson Dec 25, 1851

John Knox m. Margaret A. McSherry Mar 1, 1854

Helen Knox m. Andrew Marshall Sep 22, 1859

Sarah M. Knox m. Benjamin Marshall Nov 20, 1860

Euphemia M. Knox m. E. T. Rinehart Dec 26, 1860

Charles McClean Knox m. Meta R. Mason May 12, 1864

Elizabeth Harriet Knox m. S. Johnston Rankin Mar 17, 1868

Martha Virginia Knox m. R. Hance Boyd Apr 26, 1864

Mary Jane Rankin, dau. of Jerry, b. Sep 23, 1875

Maria Louise Rankin, dau. of Jerry, b. June 20, 1878

Samuel Knox b. Dec 21, 1794

Margaret Knox b. Oct 9, 1803

Rachel Rebecca Knox b. Apr 19, 1822

Samuel Knox b. Oct 16, 1824

John Knox b. Jan 14, 1827

Helen Margaret Knox b. March 4, 1829

Sarah Mary Knox b. Sep 26, 1831

Euphemia Mason Knox b. Feb 28, 1834

Charles McLean Knox b. May 7, 1837

A dau. b. Feb 17, 1840

Elizabeth Harriett King b. June 7, 1841

Martha Virginia Knox b. Jan 26, 1844

Mary Helen Rinehart b. March 3, 1862

Elizabeth Watson Rankin b. Nov 29, 1868

Baby, b. Apr 13, 1871

Children of Johnston and Elizabeth Rankin

Mrs. Rebecca Knox d. May 28, 1843

Samuel Knox d. May 26, 1845

Margaret Knox d. Oct 19, 1847

A dau. d. March 7, 1840

Euphemia Mason Rinehart d. March 10, 1862

Samuel Knox, M.D., son of Samuel, d. July 18, 1887

* Even Thomas Rinehart d. June 1891

Robert Hance Boyd d. Apr 30, 1892

Helen Margaret Marshall d. Apr 1, 1893

George Marshall Scott, d. Dec 1893, son of Mamie Rinehart and William Scott

E. H. Scott b. June 7, 1841

E. H. Scott m. S. Johnston Rankin March 17, 1868

Elizabeth Watson Rankin, dau. of Samuel Johnston and Elizabeth Knox Rankin, b. Nov 29, 1868

Margaret Johnston Rankin, infant dau. of Samuel Johnston and Elizabeth Knox Rankin, b. Feb 13, 1871

John Knox, son of Samuel Knox and Margaret Witherow, d. June 20, 1898

Rachel Rebecca Knox Marshall d. Apr 19, 1908

Mary Jane Rankin, dau. of Jere C. Rankin and Anna L. Huber b. Sep 23, 1875

Maria Louise Rankin, dau. of Jere C. Rankin and Annie L. Rankin b. June 20, 1878

Samuel Johnston Rankin, son of James Clark and Elizabeth W. Rankin b. June 5, 1833 and d. Dec 21, 1891

** Jere Clark Rankin, son of James C. and Elizabeth W. Rankin, d. Nov 2, 1895 and b. June 16, 1845

Maria Lorrie, dau, b. June 20, 1878

Charles McLean Knox d. Feb 19, 1894

William Witherow m. Sarah McGinley and they had a son Samuel who m. Rachel McLean and their dau. m. Samuel Knox March 15, 1821

Samuel Knox b. Dec 21, 1794 and d. May 26, 1845

Margaret Witherow Knox b. Oct 9, 1803 and d. Oct 19, 1847. Their children were:

Rachel Rebecca b. Apr 19, 1822, m. Hon. James H. Marshall Dec 5, 1842.

Samuel, M.D. b. Oct 16, 1824, m. D. Culbertson Dec 23, 1851 and d. July 18, 1887.

John b. Jan 14, 1827, m. Margaret McHenry March 1, 1854 and d. June 20, 1898.

Helen Margaret b. March 11, 1829, m. Sep 22, 1859 Andrew Marshall and d. Apr 1, 1893.

Sarah Mary b. Sep 26, 1831, m. Benjamin A. Marshall Nov 20, 1860; also m. D. Bruce Blythe, 1898.

* Samuel Johnston Rankin d. Dec 21, 1891

** Mary Jane Rankin, dau. of Jerry, b. Sep 23, 1875

No. 6. Hager Family Bible (1850).

Jacob Heager m. Miss Susan M. Pritchard 1895.

No. 8. Wilken Boyer and Ann Boyer Bible -- 1846.

Wilken Boyer and Ann Maria Phesant m. Sep 21, 1837.

Wilken Boyer b. Sep 27, 1816

Ann Maria Boyer b. Feb 25, 1816

David Boyer b. Nov 3, 1839

Wilken Boyer d. Nov 10, 1900

Ann Maria Boyer d. Feb 11, 1906

No. 9. Hager Family Bible.

James Thornton Hager b. Nov 24, 1851 at Hagerstown, Md.

Mary Du Bois Hall b. Nov 7, 1850 at Warren, Trimbull County, OH.

Mary T. Spielman d. Jan 7, 1881.

Arutha d. June 26, 1883.

No. 10. Windser Family Bible.

Newman Windser and his wife Fanny Windser m. Aug 12, 1813

Edward M. Meeley and Elizabeth Franley Windser his wife m. Nov 11, 1841

Edward Windser Meuley and Laura Gertrude Parks m. June 1, 1876

Edward Windser Meeley and Adelaide Berry Allderdice m. Oct 15, 1898

Norman Windser b. Dec 20, 1789

Fanny Windser b. Aug 29, 1790

Richard S. Windser b. Jan 8, 1816

Robert N. Windser b. May 4, 1818

Elizabeth F. Windser b. Mar 15, 1820

Joseph R. Windser b. Dec 19, 1821

John H. Windser b. Aug 5, 1824

Emily C. Windser b. June 1, 1827

Edward Windser b. Aug 23, 1846

Joseph Albert A. Mealey b. Sep 24, 1848

Richard Clinton Mealey b. June 17, 1850

Frederick Lawson Mealey b. March 12, 1852

Hannah b. March 10, 1794

Jefre b. March 27, 1796
Jordan b. Aug 29, 1804
Agness b. Jan 8, 1806
Ralph b. Dec 20, 1809
Frielin b. Nov 12, 1810
Mary b. Feb 10, 1814
Sindy b. May 20, 1814
Jiles b. July 17, 1817
Jerry b. March 12, 1819
Ritter b. Apr 29, 1820
George b. June 20, 1822
Ephriam b. Oct 7, 1824
Lewis b. Feb 18, 1827
Ely b. Nov 25, 1828
Lisa b. March 31, 1830
Fannie Windser d. Dec 21, 1828
John H. Windser d. Sep 1824
Newman Windser d. March 29, 1830
Joseph Windser d. Dec 25, 1835
Elizabeth Frances (Windser) Mealey d. July 2, 1891
Edward Windser Mealey d. Apr 28, 1911
Joseph Albert Mealey d. Apr 13, 1854
Richard Clinton Mealey d. Apr 26, 1854
Frederick Lawson Mealey d. March 25, 1856
Edward Mealey, husband of Elizabeth Frances (Windser) Mealey d. May 26, 1871
Laura Gertrude (Parks) Mealey d. Sep 20, 1897

No. 12. Sherrick & Newcomer Family Bible.

Joseph Sherrick m. Sarah Ham Apr 17, 1828
Victor H. Newcomer m. Mary H. Sherrick May 20, 1858
Virginia Sherrick Newcomer m. John L. Nicodemus Nov 9, 1892
John Luther Nicodemus b. Dec 8, 1828 and d. July 30, 1915

Virginia S. Nicodemus d. June 20, 1924

Joseph Sherrick b. Nov 12, 1801

Sarah Ham b. Jan 18, 1807

Anna Sherrick b. June 22, 1836

Victor H. Newcomer b. Sep 16, 1833

Virginia Sherrick Newcomer b. March 21, 1859

Frank Sherrick b. June 8, 1863

Barbara Sherrick d. Nov 11, 1840

Joseph Sherrick d. March 17, 1846

Jacob Sherrick b. March 2, 1798 and d. Aug 25, 1857

No. 13. Poffenberger Family Bible.

Joseph Poffenberger m. Mary Ann Kauffman Feb 8, 1838

Joseph Poffenberger b. July 26, 1812

Mary Ann Kauffman b. Oct 23, 1817

Born to Casper E. Kight and Vera Frye Kight: Theodore J. Kight b. Nov 2, 1919 at Keyser W. Va.; Casper E. Kight, Jr., b. Apr 8, 1926, at Piedmont W. Va.

George W. Frye b. Apr 12, 1855

Martha E. Frye b. Apr 7, 1842

William Clayton Frye b. Nov 12, 1863

John Ashton Nickles b. Oct 6, 1865

Angeline Frye b. Feb 12 1868

Catharine Girmettee, dau. of George W. and Martha E. Frye b. Dec 3, 1870

John Ashton Nicholas b. Oct 6, 1865 and d. March 22, 1867

Martha E. Frye b. Apr 7, 1842 and d. Sep 24, 1845

George W. Frye b. Apr 12, 1838; d. Feb 19, 1872

William Clayton Frye b. Nov 19, 1863

Susie Belle Whaley, b. Feb 10, 1868

Walter Clayton Frye b. July 21, 1889, son of Clayton & Susie Frye

Isabella Martha Frye b. June 7, 1891

Vira Frye b. Aug 13, 1893

William Clayton Frye d. Nov 5, 1898 at Newark, Ohio

Susie Frye Cooper d. Feb 19, 1925 at Newark, Ohio, buried at Monroeville, Ohio.

Isabelle M. Frye d. Feb 20, 1949 at Keyser W. Va., buried at Monroeville, Ohio.

Geary A. Cooper d. Dec 22, 1851 at Morgantown, W. Va., buried at Monroeville, Ohio.

Walter Clayton Frye d. Nov 26, 1952 at Morgantown, W. Va., buried Monroeville, Ohio.

(This bible was found on Antietam battlefield by a cabinet maker of Loudoun Co., W. Va. Before his death he gave it to his foster son William Clayton Frye.)

William Clayton Frye (Nov 19, 1863 - Nov 5, 1898). William Clayton Frye at age 17 went to Ohio in 1880 to work for B & O Railroad. At his death it went to his daughter Vira Frye. The family then moved to W. Va., thence to Maryland. In 1961 Mrs.Vira Frye Kight gave the bible to her daughter-in-law, Mrs. Casper Kight, as she was living in Hagerstown near Antietam Battlefield. (Thus in 100 years it has come the full circle.)

No. 14. Welty Family Bible.

Michael Welty m. Aug 22, 1839

David Welty b. May 25, 1841

William Geary Welty b. June 20, 1841

Rachel Ann Welty b. July 1, 1843

Sarah Elen Welty b. June 21, 1846

Martain Welty b. Aug 22, 1850

William Alforde Welty b. Oct 8, 1853

Michael Welty b. Sep 7, 1814

Amelia Welty b. Apr 10, 1816

Michael Welty d. Oct 24, 1889, age 75 years, 27 days

Martin Luther Welty d. March 29, 1896, age 45 yrs, 7 mos., 7 days.

No. 15. Eichelberger Bible.

Mrs. Barbara Eichelberger d. Apr 11, 1833, age 67 yrs

Theobold Eichelberger d. Nov 6, 1845, age 83 yrs

No. 17. Turner Bible.

John D. Turner of Washington County, Md. and Martha Pittenger m. Apr 24, 1879

No. 18. Boone and Fague Bible.

Joseph Neikirk and Mary Ellen Fague m. at Boonsboro Apr 19, 1864

Joseph Neikirk b. Jan 18, 1836

Mary Ellen Fague b. Apr 27, 1840

Children of Joseph and Mary Ellen Neikirk:
Ernest Boone b. Oct 24, 1868
Harry Wilson b. June 15, 1870
Grace May b. Apr 25, 1872
Albert Russell b. Sep 24, 1874
William Fague b. May 29, 1878
Ellen Catherine b. Mar 11, 1881
George Roy b. Oct 5, 1883

William Fague Neikirk d. Aug 15, 1878

Joseph Neikirk d. Aug 17, 1897

A. Russell Neikirk d. Feb 1914 in Colorado from a fall in a mine. His home was in Denver.

Catherine Boon b. June 8, 1814

Mary Catharine Fague b. Dec 3, 1874

John Fague Boon b. Dec 24, 1816; d. Oct 1, 1886

Catharine Fague d. Sep 30, 1902

Willard F. Fague d. Aug 5, 1864, age 8 yrs

Edward E. Fague d. Aug 14, 1871, age 24 yrs, 4 mos., 26 days

William Boon Fague d. July 7, 1876, age 26 yrs, 10 mos., 13 days

John Fague d. Oct 1, 1886

Sue M. Myers d. Feb 27, 1888

Mary Aileen Myers b. Feb 25, 1875

Milbrey Strite Myers b. Sep 11, 1865

No. 19. Benjamin H. Latrobe Bible.

Benjamin H. Latrobe and Juliana Eleanor Hazelhurst m. March 12, 1833 in Salem, N.J.

Charles H. Latrobe and Letitia B., dau. of Col.. Robert Gamble m. at Tallahassee, Florida Apr 2, 1861

Agnes Catherine Latrobe and Cornelius Weston m. at Emmanuel Church, Baltimore, July 9, 1867

Mary Elizabeth Latrobe and Henry Onderdonk m. at Emmanuel Church, Baltimore Dec 17, 1868

Charles H. Latrobe and Rosa W. Robinson, dau. of Dr. A. C. Robinson m. at Grace Church, Baltimore, Dec 14, 1869

Benjamin H. Latrobe Jr. and Jenny Estette Yeater m. Dec 2, 1873

Charles Hazlehurst b. Dec 25, 1833 in Baltimore

Edward Latrobe b. May 31, 1835 in Salem, N. J.

Mary Elizabeth Latrobe b. Aug 27, 1836

Agnes Catherine Latrobe b. Dec 25, 1838 in Baltimore

Benjamin Henry Latrobe b. Dec 4, 1840 in Baltimore

Maria Eleanor Latrobe b. Oct 8, 1843 in Baltimore

Elsie Gamble Latrobe, dau. of Charles H. and Letitia B. Latrobe, b. May 6, 1863, in Tallahassee, Fla.

Eleanor Breckenridge Latrobe b. Oct 6, 1864, Tallahassee, Fla.

Gamble Latrobe, son of C. H. and L. B. Latrobe, b. June 21, 1866 in Baltimore

Benjamin Latrobe Weston, son of Cornelius and Kate Weston, b. Sep 8, 1868, in Baltimore

Henry Bancroft Weston, son of above, b. Jan 1, 1871 in Balto.

Benjamin Latrobe Onderdonk, son of Henry and Mary E. Latrobe Onderdonk, b. May 12, 1872 at St. James College

Arthur Hazelhurst Weston, son of Cornelius and Kate Weston, b. Aug 18, 1872 at St. James College

Laurason Riggs Latrobe, son of Rev. B. H. Latrobe, Jr., b. March 25, 1875, in Baltimore

No. 22. Speck Family Bible.

John M. Walker m. Eliza Poisal Dec 16, 1828

Martin Speck m. Nancy Spickler Oct 16, 1810

David Anderson m. Mary Speck Sep 13, 1836

John Hicks m. Elizabeth Speck Jan 28, 1840

David Speck m. Rebecca Stouffer, Dec 28, 1843

Martin Speck m. Isabella Pittinger Feb 8, 1840

Catherine Speck m. Daniel Middlekauff March 12, 1867 [or 1861?]

Margaret Speck m. Joseph Hershey Mar 24, 1863

Samuel Speck m. Elizabeth Jacobs Apr 21, 1863

John M. Walker b. Jan 11, 1805

Eliza Walker b. Nov 22, 1810

Margaret E. Walker b. Nov 6, 1829

John P. Walker b. Jan 12 1831

Martin Speck, son of William, b. Nov 15, 1789

Nancy Speck b. July 24, 1790

Mary Speck b. Apr 15, 1811

Elizabeth Speck b. Aug 28, 1812

Susannah Speck b. Jan 20, 1815

Martin Speck b. Jan 3, 1817

Frederick Speck b. Dec 12, 1818

Catharine Speck b. Feb 1, 1821

David Speck b. Apr 5, 1823

Peter Speck b. Jan 11, 1825

Nancy Speck b. Feb 8, 1827

Samuel Speck b. June 3, 1829

Margaret Speck b. July 6, 1832

Susanna Speck d. Jan 20, 1824, age 10 yrs, 10 mos.

Martin Speck, Sr., d. March 24, 1852, age 62 yrs, 9 days.

Ann Speck d. Oct 21, 1858, age 68 yrs, 2 mos., 20 days.

Martin Speck d. Apr 11, 1877

Isabella Speck d. Jan 20, 1878

Polly Speck d. Dec 22, 1892, in Tiffen, Ohio.

Peter Speck d. Jan 9, 1896 in Tiffen, Ohio.

Elizabeth Speck d. Oct 15, 1898

David Speck d. June 19, 1900 near Cearfoss, age 77

Mrs. Mary Anderson d. Feb 1, 1901

Mrs. Catherine Flook d. Dec 7, 1902

Mrs. Nannie Myer, d. Apr 6, 1903

Frederick Speck d. Jan 14, 1905, age 86 yrs

Samuel Speck d. Dec 16, 1905, age 76 yrs, 6 mos., 13 days

No. 24. Shiefler Family Bible.

George Shiefler, b. Feb 7, 1824

No. 26. Henry A. Bachtel Bible, donated by Mrs. Chester Clark.

John Jacob Bachtel b. March 6, 1750

Catharine Letch, his wife, b. Apr 15, 1755. They m. March 16, 1773. Their children were:

John Jacob Bachtel, Jr., b. Feb 10, 1774

George Bachtel b. Oct 14, 1775

Magdalene Bachtel b. Dec 3, 1777

Jacob Bachtel (my grandfather) b. Oct 9, 1779, Wash. Co.

Martin Bachtel b. Oct 26 1783, Washington Co., Md.

Anna Barbara Bachtel b. Nov 5, 1786

Frederick Bachtel b. March 21, 1789

Anna Mary Bachtel b. Nov 5,1791

David Bachtel b. Aug 28, 1793

Thomas Bachtel b. Feb 17, 1796

David Bachtel b. June 13, 1798

Pioneers of Md., Penna. and Ohio -- Harry A. Bachtel, Jan 8, 1899, 118 Prospect.

Hammacker Material

John Hubert Hammacker and his brother Adam came to America in 1740 from Rotterdam, Holland on Ship Elizabeth. Settled in Lancaster Co., Pa. descendants scattered all over Penna. Adam Hammaker born 1717 died 1784. Was the father of Adam Hammaker, a member of the Flying Camp of Penna. during the Revolutionary War. The latter's son Samuel educated at Chambersburg, Pa., married Anna Overdear who with her sister Polly came from Lancaster Co., the latter married a Mr. Miller, near Williamsport, Wash. Co., Md. and the Chicago Leiters are her descendants. Annie Miller (artist) of Williamsport is a lineal descendant. Samuel Hammaker and Anna Overdear had many children (1) Peter Hammacker, b. Jan. 11, 1792, m. Elizabeth Krouse, of Peter and Maria, b. Oct 21, 1817. They had issue:

Maria and Anna, twins, b. July 15, 1818

Ephriam, b. Aug 1821, d. Nov 15, 1880

Solomon, b. March 6, 1825, d. 1855

Sophia b. March 13, 1827, d. Aug 27, 1891

David (or Daniel) b. Nov 2, 1829, d. 1891

Henry A. Bachtel b. Apr 30, 1851, son of Samuel and Anna B.

Irene Hamill b. March 2, 1856, b. at Huyetts

Parents of Henry A. Bachtel, Samuel (born at Huyetts) b. March 21, 1814.

Anna Hammaker, dau. of Peter Hammacker and Elizabeth Krouse, b. July 15, 1818, Stoner's Mill near Waynesboro, Pa. Issue:

Jacob L. Bachtel, b. Oct 26, 1841

Peter Cornelius b. July 14, 1843

William L. b. March 22, 1845

Daniel Steward b. March 10, 1847

Mary E. b. Feb 22, 1849

Margaret Ann, b. Feb 12, 1852

Benjamin H. b. March 12, 1851 -- lived 5 days

Henry Alfred b. Apr 30, 1854

Emma S. b. at Pondsville Dec 17, 1858

Ella Sophia b. Feb 12, 1862

Henry Alfred Bachtel m. Irene Hughes Hamill at Clearspring June 25, 1879

Samuel A. Bachtel (father) m. Anna Hammaker June 21, 1840 near Cavetown

Jacob L. m. Kate Snyder at Smithsburg Jan 10, 1865

Daniel S. m. Sallie J. Richardson at Clearspring

Emma S. m. Allen Heck Oswald Dec 18, 1885

Mary E. m. Milton Witmer had not issue

Margaret A. m. Daniel Stephy Cavetown - 1895 had no issue

Issue of Daniel Steward and Sallie (J. Richardson) Bachtel:

Francis Samuel b. Nov 23, 1870
Clarence Rich b. Oct 24, 1872
William Alfred b. Feb 11, 1874
Robert Howard b. July 9, 1876
Harry Ernest b. Sep 22, 1878

Issue by second wife, widow Gerber:
Elsie lived with Aunt Margaret Stephey
Scott lived with his aunt Mary Elizabeth Witmer
Steward lived with grandparents near Cavetown

No. 28. Otho Williams Family Bible, published in 1813. Donor: Mrs. George S. Fundis, 1140 Fairview Rd., Hagerstown.

Otho Williams b. Apr 12, 1785

Otho Williams m. May 24, 1814 Catharine McDowell

Otho Williams m. Ann M. McDowell May 27, 1823

Mary Holliday Williams b. July 3, 1815

Louise Jane Williams b. July 29, 1816

Thomas Owen Williams b. May 26, 1818

Violetta Williams b. March 24, 1820

Anna McPherson Williams b. Apr 24, 1824

Mary Emma Berry Williams b. May 20, 1826; bapt. by Rev. George Keller

Anna McDowell Williams b. Feb 17, 1828

Catharine M. McDowell b. Jan 17, 1793

Agnes Miller McDowell b. March 23, 1798; bapt. by Rev. John King

Helen Margaret Williams b. Dec 2, 1829, bapt. by Rev. Isaac King

Virginia Washington Williams b. Jan 2, 1833, bapt. by Rev. Isaac Keller

Mary Holliday d. Sep 23, 1815

Catharine M. Williams d. Oct 4, 1821

Violetta Williams d. Oct 16, 1822, was 2 yrs, 6 mos., 22 days old

Anna McPherson Williams d. July 27, 1824, aged 3 mos., and 3 days

Anna McDowell Williams d. Sep 1, 1828, aged 6 weeks and 4 days

Thomas Owen Williams d. Nov 1, 1829

Helen Margaret Williams d. Aug 23, 1831

No. 29. Bible in German, printed in Basil in 1729 and purchased in Lancaster, Pa., by Johannes Nicol in 1751, Apr 9. The family name Craft is written in the book several times. The Nicol and Craft families were Washington Co. families. Donor: Mr. Edward Switzer, 305 Oak Ridge Dr., Rochester, N.Y.

Additional papers:

Diagram of Fort Duquesne with a two column poem on the verse side.

A tragedy along the Kennebeck River in 1784 with Biblical puzzle on the verse side.

Handwritten notes possibly for a sermon by Johannes Nicol.

Engravings relative to the Augsburg confession including portraits Gustav Vasa and Frederic I.

Handwritten page still to be deciphered on which the dates 1774, 1781, 1782, 1787, 1789 and 1797 are clearly visible.

A badly faded page 97 torn from a ledger at the top of which is written John   1787.

Envelop containing various handwritten records:

1. dated 1755
2. undated
3. Minute pieces with writing on both sides
4. dated 1786
5. undated
6. drawings of horses
7. minuscule bits
8. other

No. ?

Samuel Garwick b. Sep 24, 1851

Amanda Bowser b. Sep 15, 1852

Samuel Garwick d. Apr 23, 1900, aged 48 yrs, 6 mos., 29 days

No. ?

Daniel S. Shifler b. Oct 9, 1842

Maria Shifler b. June 10, 1844

Clayton Elmer Shifler b. Aug 26 1866

Clarence Lemuel Shifler b Nov 20, 1867

George Edgar Shifler b. July 4, 1869

Walter Eugene Shifler b. Nov 28, 1871

Lola Mabell Shifler b June 16, 1878

Ruannia A. Shifler b. Dec 14 1816, d. May 9, 1863, aged 46 yrs, 4 mos., 26 days.

Mrs. Susannah Nikirk b. Sep 20, 1814, d. May 16, 1866, aged 57 yrs

Mr. John Nikirk b. Dec 25, 1807, d. May 16 1878, aged 71 yrs, 4 mos., 21 days

Mrs. Maria Shifler d. Jan 22, 1897, aged 52 yrs, 7 mos., 12 days

Daniel Snyder Shifler [nothing else]

Clarence Lemuel Shifler d. June 17, 1932, aged 64 yrs, 7 mos., 7 days.

Daniel S. Shifler and Maria Nikirk m. Oct 9, 1865 by Rev L. Shufford

George E. Shifler and Leila M. Huffer m. Nov 16, 1892 by Rev. Mc-Loughen.

Clarence Lemuel Shifler and Sarah Elizabeth Fiechtig[?] m. Sep 6, 1894 by Dr. S. W. Owen

In the Mt. Carmal U.B. Church on Thurs Jan 31, 1895 Walter E. Shifler and Alice E. Miller m. by Rev E. B. C. Castle.

No. ?

A. W. Lucas and Mary Randolph (dau. of Benj. Brown) m. Sep 1, 1869

Edward Bristol Lucas d. Apr 6, 1880

James Williams Lucas d. Nov 15, 1872

No. ? Beatty and Bowie Bible. Published in Philadelphia in 1854. Sold to Mrs.Harold Beck, 1020 25th Ave. N., St. Petersburg, FL 33704. (813) 898-0974

Thomas Bowie son of John Bowie Sr. b. 1722

m. Hannah Lee 1758

Issue

Barbara Bowie b. 1759, d.1805

Mr. James Hall - issue Elizabeth Bowie Hall who m. General Otho Holland Williams. Issue Catharine L. Williams, Laura Williams, ... Williams and Maria Williams who m. Edward Beatty son of Eli Beatty who emigrated to this country. Edward Beatty joined the confederate army and was killed in the battle of Harrisonville?, Va. in 1863 - Issue Elizabeth Chew Beatty who m. Thomas Johns[?] David Bowie, Kate Beatty [?] 1859, Edward Beatty who joined the Confederate Army with his father, was captured and put in prison on Johnsons Island, Lake Erie, where he died in 1864, he was buried in Union Cemetery, Rockville, Md. - and Laura Beatty who m. ..[?] Bradley Magruder

John Bowie b. 1688 came to Maryland from Scotland in 1705. married Mary Mullikin died 1759 was buried at Brookefield, Prince George Co., Md. Issue: John Bowie Jr., Eleanor Bowie, James Bowie, Allen Bowie, William Bowie, Thomas Bowie and Mary Bowie.

John Bowie, Jr., b. 1708 m. Mary Beall. Issue: William and Milly Bowie. His second wife was Elizabeth Pottinger. Issue Allen Bowie, James Bowie, Rev. John Bowie -Died in 1753, buried at ..., PG Co. His widow married Thomas Cramphin. Died 1775 buried - in Rock Creek Cemetery.

Col. Allen Bowie, jr., b. 1736, m. Ruth Cramphin, served in the Revolutionary war, died in 1803, he and his wife buried in Union Cemetery Rockville, Md. Issue Thomas Bowie, Dr. John Bowie, Elizabeth Bowie, Mary Bowie, Washington Bowie, Allen Bowie, Hannah Bowie and Richard Bowie.

Col. Washington Bowie. b. 1776. General George Washington for whom he was named was his god father. m. Margaret Crabb and d. 1825. He and his wife were buried at Oatland near Olney, Montgomery County, Md. Issue: Thomas John Bowie, Mary Bowie, Margaret Bowie, Washington Bowie, Jr., Judge Richard Johns Bowie, Robert Gilmer Bowie and Sarah Hollyday Bowie. He was commissioned Colonel of Militia.

Col. Thomas Johns Bowie, b. 1800. m. Catharine W. Davis, d. 1850, his wife d. 1888, both buried at Oatland in private cemetery owned by the Bowies. He was commissioned Colonel of Militia. Issue: Thomas John Davis Bowie, Sarah Hollyday Bowie, Glen Ruth Bowie and Washington Bowie.

Thomas John Davis Bowie, b. 1834, d. 1921, m. Elizabeth Chew Beatty Nov 24, 1854 She d. May 25, 1868. Both buried in Union Cemetery Rockville, Md. Issue: Edward Beatty Bowie, Catharine Davis Bowie, Allen Thomas Bowie and Maria Williams Bowie.

Edward Beatty Bowie, b. 1857, m. Eleanor Voss [?] 1885, resides in Wheeling W. Va., issue: Robert Edward Bowie and Allen Davis Bowie.

Robert Edward Bowie, b. 1886, m. Ednor Mary Kidd.

Allen Davis Bowie b. 1885 [1895?], m. Virginia Jacobs. Issue: Mary Eleanor Bowie ...[?]

Catharine Davis Bowie, b. 1859 m. James E.[?] Trindle [?]

Allen Thomas Bowie, b. 1861 m. Mary Baul [Beall?] 1893. He died Feb 4, 1914, buried Union Cemetery Rockville, Md. Issue Georgia Paull[?] Bowie, m. Henry Hazlett. Issue: Mary Beall Hazlett b. 1917; Maria ...[?] Bowie, b. July 21, 1893

"Affectionally compiled for Munnie W. Bowie by her devoted Uncle Washington Bowie, May 1921."

Elizabeth C. Bowie d 25 May 1868 at Flinthill, near Mechanicsville, Montgomery Co., Md. and was interred in the cemetery attached to St. Johns church. Afterward moved to Union Cemetery, Rockville, Md.

Thomas Johns Bowie d on the [blank] of Feb 1921.

Allen Thomas Bowie d. Feb 4, 1914

Edward Beatty Bowie d. May 7, 1929.

Catharine Davis Bowie d. Jan 4, 1942.

MARRIAGES

Elizabeth Chew Beatty, Thomas John Davis Bowie m. in St. Johns Church, Hagerstown, Maryland, Nov 21, 1855, by Revd. Walter Ayrault.

Edward Beatty Bowie - Eleanor Vars [Vass, Bass?] Dec 9, 1885.

Robert Edward Bowie, Edna Kidd Dec 10, 1917.

Allen Thomas Bowie and Mary Paull 1893.

Thomas John Davis Bowie son of Thomas John Bowie and Catharine

BIRTHS

McBr...[?] b. Jan 23, 1834.

Elizabeth Chew Beatty, dau. of Edward W. Beatty and Maria A. Beatty, b. Apr 26, 1835.

Edward Beatty Bowie, son of Thomas John Davis Bowie and Elizabeth his wife, b. June 18, 1857.

Catharine Davis Bowie, dau. of Thomas J. D. Bowie and Elizabeth his wife, b. Jan 31, 1859.

Allen Thomas Bowie, second son of Thomas J. D. Bowie and Elizabeth his wife b. Nov 7, 1861.

Maria Williams Bowie second dau. of Thomas J. D. Bowie and Elizabeth his wife, b. July 21, 1863.

Bible Records of Henry A. Bachtell. Pub. by A. J. Johnson, 11 Great Jones Street, New York, 1874.

Family Record, original in German, now in English. Jan 2, 1897.

The possession of Moses A. Bachtel (father's coz in Canton, Ohio)

John Jacob Bachtel b. March 6, 1750.

Catharine Letch his wife b. Apr 15, 1755 and m. March 16, 1773. Lived also in Conamaughville, near Johnstown, Penna.

Children:

John Jacob Bachtel b. Feb 10, 1774, eldest John
George Bachtel b. Oct 14, 1775
Magdalene Bachtel b. Dec 3, 1777
John Jacob Bachtel (my grandfather) b. Oct 9, 1779, Md. Wash. Co.
Jno. Martin Bachtel b. Oct 26, 1783, Md., Wash. Co.
Anna Barbara Bachtel Nov 5, 1786
Frederick Bachtel b. March 21, 1789
Anna Mary Bachtel b. Nov 5, 1791
Daniel Bachtel b. Aug 28, 1793
Thomas Bachtel b. Feb 17, 1796
David Bachtel b. June 13, 1798

Pioneers of Md. Penna. and Ohio

Psalms LXXIV - 5

"A man was famous according as he lifted up axes upon the thick trees."
Hy. A. Bachtel, 118 Prospect St., Hagerstown, Md. Jan 8, 1899.

Ancestors of Irene H. Bachtel (nee Hamill)

Wm. Hamill m. Dorcas Galbraith Oct 1, 1812. Parents of Dr. S. B. Hamill and grandparents of Irene. (Buried at Falling Waters)

Children:

Mary Hamill b. Sep 9, 1816. Sec. husband Armstrong D. C. died Shippensburg 1893. (1890 now living with step-sister Elenor Wigdon, Spring Garden., Phila.)

Robert Hamill b. Apr 19, 1816, m. Jane Royer; son Royer Hamil, wife Carrie Pattons, cousin to Ingram's wife, near Cavetown

Wm. Hamill's second wife - Rebecca Ashman, b. Feb 14, 1790, m. Apr 2, 1818.

Children to Wm. and 2nd wife:

Ashman Hamill, Oct 9, 1819, Martinsburg

Wm. Cromwell Hamill, Aug 1821

Eliz. Hamill July 1823

Eleanor Hamill Apr 29, 1827, m. R. Benton Wigton, Phila., d. 1895.

Rebecca Hamill Apr 10, 1830

George Hamill minor son of Jas. & Mary Hamill b. Jef. Co., Va., Oct 7, 1823

Dr. E. B. Hamill son of Wm. and Rebecca was mar.

Dr. E. B. Hamill m. Irene Hughes Nov 22, 1853/Mary Eliz. b. 12-15-1854, Irene Hughes, Mar 2, 1856. Mary Eliz. m. March 9, 1875 Capt. W. Bullen; their children (Sallie died, Bessie died, Fannie died). Irene Hughes m. June 25, 1879 Prof. H. A. Bachtel, no issue.

May 24, 1859, Mary Cath. Hooper died Jan 16, 1897 Martinsburg, buried Greencastle.

Apr 5, 1860 Geo. A. Hamill

Belle A. Hamill mar. H. S. Taylor of Willoughby, Ohio a boy Hammill

Dr. Geo. A., Martinsburg, Va., 1882

Miss Banton, Sharpsburg, 3 children, 1 girl, 1895

Dr. Geo. Ashman Hamill, Dentist, D. D. S., Martinsburg, W. Va. died Apr 1901, aged 45. Widow and daughter are with aunt Mrs. Showman. Dr. Hamill was the leading dentist in W. Va. as was his father Dr. E. B. Hamill during his lifetime.

Family Record Miscellaneous

Issue of Daniel Stewart and Sallie J. Richardson:

Francis Samuel B. Nov 22, 1870

Clarenc Rich. b. Oct 24, 1872

Wm. Alfred b. Feb 11, 1874

Robert Howard b. July 19, 1876

Harry Earnest b. Sep 22, 1878

Issue by second wife, widow Gerber (nee Ill. Souders) m. Dec 19, 1883 died

11 yrs, Elsio with her aunt Margaret Stephey

9 yrs Scott with his aunt Mary Eliz. Witmer

6. Stewart with his grandparents near Cavetown

Stewart, Jr. and Howard were constant companions at the bedside of their grandfather during his last illness.

Family Record - Births

Henry A. Bachtel, son of Samuel and Anna B., b. Apr 30, 1854, A. D.

Irene H. Hamill, of Dr. E. B. Hamill, b. March 2, 1856 A. D.

Parents of Hy. A. Bachtel

Samuel A. Bachtell, b. March 21, 1814, at Huyett's, now owned by Joshua Houck, (1895)

Anna Hammaker (Peter Hammaker & Eliz. Krouse), b. July 15, 1818, at Stoner's Mill, near Waynesboro, Pa.

Issue:

Jacob L. b. Oct 26, 1841, at Grandfather's (Hammaker) farm, near Shank's church

Peter Cornelius, b. July 14, 1843, at Beard's Farm, Chewsville

Wm. L. B. March 22, 1845, on Peter Krouse farm, near Cavetown, Md.

Danl. Stewart b. March 10, 1847

Mary E. b. Feb 22, 1849

Benj. H. b. March 12, 1851, lived 5 days

Margaret Ann b. Feb 12, 1852 at Desert Farm, Beard's Church

Henry Alfred b. Apr 30, 1854, above Cavetown

Emma S. b. Dec 17, 1858, at Pondsville

Ellen Sophia b. Feb 12, 1862, born near present house, now Geo. Noel's, Cavehill, lived there during Civil War

Family Record - Marriages

Henry Alfred Bachtell m. Irene Hughes Hamill June 25, 1879 by Rev. C. R. Page, at Clear Spring, Md.

Samuel A. Bachtell (father) m. Anna Hammaker, Jan 21, 1840 near Cavetown, Wash. Co., Md. Lived 28 yrs.

Jacob L. (bro) m. Kate Snyder, Jan 10, 1865, at Smithsburg, sister to Frisby Stouffer

Danl. S. m. Sallie Richardson, Holden, Mo.

Henry A. m. Irene Hughes Hamill June 25, 1879 at Clear Spring, Md.

Emma S. to Allen Heck Oswald Dec 18, 1885

Mary E. to Milton Witmer, Beaver Creek, no issue

Margaret A. to Daniel Stephey, Cavetown, Md. no issue 1895

Family Records - Deaths

Samuel Augusta Bachtell (father) d. March 22, 1895, aged 81 yrs and 1 day, near Cavetown, Md. Grandsons, Howard, Stewart and Harry were present.

Benjamin F. d. March 17, 1851, aged 5 days

Ellen Sophia d. March 16, 1863 or 64.

Peter C. d. July 16, 1865

Sallie J. Richardson, wife of Danl. S. d. Aug 25, 1880

Anna Hammaker Krouse Bachtell d. Apr 6, 1900 near Cavetown, Md.

Fly leaves in rear of Bible

Maternal ancestors of Henry A. Bachtel

Mother Anna Hammaker b. at Ingram's Mill near Smithsburg, Md. They lived there 8 yrs. Moved to Mill near Welty's Church for 2 years. Then to Singer's Mill above Ringgold for 2 yrs. Then to Stoner's Mill near Waynesboro. Was there many years, attended school. Her twin sister married Saul (Samuel?) Royer. She was Mary. He taught school. Moved to Beard's Church on Harrys farm which they (grandfather) purchased for $50 an acre in 1839. He died about 1841 when it was sold for $70 an acre. They purchased the farm near Shank's School House where mother was married and lived several years. Jacob, oldest sons was born here. Died 1873, aged 78.

Maternal Grandmother was Eliz. Krouse. Krouse came to Md. an emigrant from Germany, landed in Baltimore 1788 aged 15 born 1773. M. a Miss Wolf, 1805. d. 1843, buried Beard's Church.

Maternal grandparents - Elizabeth Krouse & Peter Hammaker

Children - Ephraim, Mary twins, Anna, Solomon, Sophia, died Cavetown, 1890; Daniel, died Pondsville, 1898

Eph[raim] m. Susan Shank. Children: Adam, Peter, Amanda m. Snavely, Saml., Stewart, Lizzie.

Mary m. Saml. Royer. Children: Dan., Jno., Thos., Mary m. Nichols, Lizzie, ?? to Nichol, Ella to Wassler.

2nd fly leaf - Hammaker's (Maternal)

John Hubrect Hamaker and Adam brothers came to America in 1740 from Rotterdam, Holland on ship "Elizabeth." Settled in Lebanon Co., Penna. and descendants scattered all over Pa. Adam Hamaker b. 1717, d. 1784 was the father of Adam, a member of the Flying Camp of Penna. during the Revolutionary War. The latter's son Samuel educated at Chambersburg, Penna., married Anna Overdear, who with her sister Polly, came from Lancaster Co. The latter married a Mr. Miller near Wmsport, Wash. Co., Md., and the Chicago Leiters are her descendants. Annie Miller (artist) of Williamsport is a lineal descendant.

Samuel Hamaker and Anna Overdear had many children. Peter Hammaker born Jan 11, 1792, married Elizabeth Krouse of Peter and Mary. b. July 31, 1795. m. Oct 21, 1817. Issue: d. 1888 [sic]; Maria & Anna (twins) b. July 15, 1818; Ephraim b. Aug 1821, d. 11-15-1880; Solomon b. Mar 6, 1825, d. 1855; Sophia b. Mar 13, 1827, d. Aug 27, 1891; Danl. b. Nov 2, 1829, d. 1898.

Blee Family Holy Bible - Births

Willis Blackwell Blee, b. Jan 21, 1881

Ralph Carroll Blee, b. March 8, 1883

Mary Edna Blee, b. May 15, 1887

From a page loose from a Bible.

Submitted by Ellen Ardinger Zeller, National #3431110

Mrs. Dennis T. Zeller, 1329 The Terrace, Hagerstown, Md.

Copied for Conococheague Chapter, NSDAR, Hagerstown, Md. by Mrs. Samuel L. Greenawalt, Librarian and Chairman of Genealogical Records, 1968.

Bowser Family Holy Bible

Bible in possession of Jane Bowser Fahnestock (Mrs. Luis Fahnestock, III), 725 Fountain Head Rd., N., Hagerstown, Md.

"Grandfather and Grandmother Bowser"

William Oscar Bowser, b. Dec 12, 1850; d. June 6, 1926

m. Jan 20, 1874, by Pastor Owens in St. John's Lutheran Church of Hagerstown, Md. to Hannah Ardinger, b. March 16, 1853; d. Aug 22, 1937 Children: 1. Bertie Imo Hawken, b. Dec 1, 1874; d. Aug 31, 1958. 2. Oscar Owens Bowser, b. March 12, 1876; d. March 5, 1879. 3. Jonathan Peter Bowser, b. May 19, 1878; d. June 18, 1956. 4. Meda or Meta Herbert Earnshaw, b. July 6, 1881; d. Oct 4, 1948. 5. Katie Roessner Bowser, b. March 10, 1885. 6. William Maurice Bowser, b. March 18, 1887; d. July 11, 1887. 7. Judith Irene Bowser, b. Sep 18, 1889; d. Jan 27, 1890. 8. Agnes Louise Bowser, b. Dec 4, 1890; d. March 4, 1891.

Copied by Ellen Ardinger Zeller (Mrs. Dennis T. Zeller), National #431110, 1329 The Terrace, Hagerstown, Md. Copied for Conococheague Chapter, NSDAR, by Mrs. Samuel Greenawalt.

Gardner Family Holy Bible

H. S. Goodspeed & Co., New York & Chicago, 1872

Marriages

Mr. William Gardner and Miss Mary Scott of Greencastle, Pa. were united in Matrimony by Rev. B. Bridenbaugh, Oct 28, in the year 1858.

Births

William Gardner was b. March 29, 1823; d. July 26, 1893

Mary Scott was born June 30, 1824; d. Dec 15, 1891.

Thomas Jefferson Gardner was b. Jan 31, 1850; d. Nov 18, 1910.

Anna Rebecca Gardner was b. Feb 14, 1859; d. Aug 1, 1859

Ida Florence Gardner was b. Apr 30, 1861; d. Feb 22, 1934

Mary Catherine (Mollie) Gardner was b. Feb 24, 1865; d. 195-

Alice Viola Gardner was b. Aug 14, 1868

William Earl Gardner was b. May 13, 1893; d. Sep 15, 1934

Deaths

Theresa Scott d. Aug 28, 1927

Viola Florence Gardner Upperman d. March 11, 1952

Elizabeth Smith Gardner d. Sep 12, 1866

John Gardner d. Feb 5, 1864

David Gardner d. Feb 17, 1896

Mrs. Elizabeth Gardner Byers d. Feb 24, 1898, 79 yrs. 5 mo. 29 da.

William Gardner d. July 26, 1893

Bible owned by Ellen Ardinger Zeller (Mrs. Dennis T.) National #431110, 1329 The Terrace, Hagerstown, Md. Submitted by above for Conococheague Chapter, NSDAR.

Family Bible of Joseph Garrish

Joseph Garrish of Williamsport, Md., and Georgietta Ardinger of Williamsport, Md. were united in Holy Matrimony at Cumberland, Md., on Oct 20, 1873, by Austin M. Courtney, Bedford St. M.E. Ch. Mrs. Alice McCardell & J. J. Valiant, Witnesses.

Children of Joseph & Georgietta Garrish: 1. Sprigg Dixon Garrish, b. Oct 19, 1874. 2. Joseph Benjamin Garrish, b. Dec 24, 1875. 3. George Jacob Garrish, b. Oct 9, 1877. 4. Lutie Albert Garrish, b. Sep 14, 1879; d. Aug 24, 1881 aged 1 yr., 11 mo. 10 da. 5. Clara Elizabeth Garrish, b. Sep 26, 1881. 6. Ellen Steward Garrish, b. Nov 20, 1883; d. July 18, 1885 aged 1 yr, 7 mo., 18 da. 7. Maggie Thompson Garrish, b. Sep 23, 1885. 8. Isaac Thompson Garrish, b. Sep 24, 1887. 9. Bruce William Garrish, b. Oct 1, 1889. 10. Lewis E. McComas Garrish, b. July 18, 1891. 11. Frank Thomas Goddard Garrish, b. June 10, 1893. 12. Isabell Ridell Garrish, b. May 16, 1895. 13. Florence K. Garrish, b. Apr 10, 1897; d. Feb 22, 1902 aged 5 yr., 5 da. 14. Osman Latrobe Garrish, b. March 16, 1899. 15. Thomas Rhodes Garrish, b. Oct 17, 1901.

Joseph Henry Garrish was b. Feb 14, 1844

Georgietta Garrish was b. Oct 27, 1856.

Bible in possession of Ellen Ardinger Zeller (Mrs. Dennis Zeller) of Williamsport, Md. and Hagerstown, Md. Copied for Conococheague Chapter, NSDAR, Hagerstown, Md. by Mary Burgner Greenawalt (Mrs. Samuel L. Greenawalt).

Hayman Family Holy Bible

Bible in possession of Margaretta Hayman (Mrs. Edgar T. Hayman), Wilson's, Route #2, Hagerstown, Md. Nov 1967.

Mary Hanna, b. Apr 15, 1786, White Hall, Washington Co., Md.; d. Apr 21, 1869, Washington Co., Md.; m. Dec 30, 1807 to John Brinham, b. June 2, 1774, St. Mary's Co., Md.; d. March 17, 1855, Washington Co., Md.

Children: 1. Sarah Ann Brinham, b. May 7, 1809, Washington Co., Md.; d. May 7, 1889, Kittaning, Pa., m. Apr 16, 1827 to Benjamin Oswald, b. July 10, 1802; d. March 17, 1855, Kittaning, Pa. 2. James Brinham, b. Jan 17, 1811, Washington Co., Md.; d. Aug 27, 1846, Washington Co., Md. 3. John Randolph Birnham, b. Dec 12, 1812, Washington Co., Md.; d. Jan 11, 1892; m. Sep 18, 1840 to Ann Winters, b. Apr 26, 1817; d. Apr 29, 1892. 4. Nancy Brinham, b. Dec 5, 1814, Washington Co., Md.; d. Feb 10, 1895, Washington Co., Md., never married. 5. Elizabeth Brinham, b. Feb 3, 1817; d. 1898, b. & d. Washington Co., Md. not married. 6. Mary Brinham, b. March 16, 1819, Washington Co., Md.; m. Jan 31, 1838 to Thomas McAtee, moved to Polo, Ill. 7. Margaretta Brinham, b. Sep 6, 1821; d. Oct 27, 1897; (m., b. & d. Washington Co., Md.) m. Jan 10, 1843 to Daniel Huyett, b. Feb 6, 1823; d. May 31, 1905, Washington Co., Md. 8. Jane Brinham, b. Dec 21, 1823, Washington Co., Md.; d. Dec 21, 1915, aged 92 yrs. Buried Rose Hill Cemetery, Hagerstown, Md., m. Dec 14, 1848 to Jacob Wolfkill, b. Oct 22, 1825, Beaver Creek, Md.; d. March 2, 1884, Washington Co., Md. Buried Rose Hill Cemetery. 9. George Washington Brinham, b. Jan 15, 1826, Washington Co., Md; d. Apr 25, 1896 in Washington, Co., Md. never married. 10. Benjamin Brinham, b. Nov 14, 1827; d. Feb 15, 1903; m. Sep 4, 1854 to Mary E. Martin, b. June 2, 1832; d. Dec 9, 1909 - all born, married & died in Washington Co., Md.

11. America Brinham, b. Sep 20, 1930, Washington Co., Md.; d. Jan 22, 1897; m. 1st Jacob Harbaugh Feb 28, 1854; b. Aug 16, 1820; d. June 11, 1877; m. 2nd Henry McCauley

12. Ellen Brinham, b. Aug 27, 1833, Washington Co., Md.; d. Jan 15, 1924, Washington Co., Md.; m. Dec 12, 1855 to Martin Geiser, b. May 14, 1828; d. Apr. 1898, b. & d. Washington Co., Md. Buried Waynesboro, Pa. Cemetery.

Copied from records of Mrs. Edgar T. Hayman by Ellen Ardinger Zeller (Mrs. Dennis T. Zeller), National #431110, 1329 The Terrace, Hagerstown, Md. Copied for Conococheague Chapter, NSDAR, Hagerstown, Md. by Mrs. Samuel L. Greenawalt, Chapter Librarian, 1967.

Mary Hanna, child of John Hanna

John Hanna, b. Oct 26, 1748, Chester Co., Pa.; d. May 4, 1838, Washington Co., Md.; m. Ann (Nancy) MacDill 1779 at Chester Co., Pa., b. 1775, Chester Co., Pa.; d. May 25, 1847, Washington Co., Md.

Bible Records - Samuel Knox Family

Holy Bible - Printed by American Bible Society, N.Y., 1854

This Bible is now in possession of Washington County Historical Society, Hagerstown, Maryland.

MARRIAGES

Samuel Knox to Margaret Witherow, by Rev. John King D.D., on March 15, 1821.

Rachel Rebecca Knox, dau. of Samuel to James H. Marshall, Dec 5, 1842 by Rev. John Knox D.D. of New York City.

Samuel Knox to Mary E. Culbertson by Rev. Jos. Mason, Dec 23, 1851.

John Knox to Margaret A. McSherry by Rev. David Clark, March 1, 1854.

Helen M. Knox to Andrew Marshall, Sep 22, 1859, by Rev. J. R. Warner.

Sarah M. Knox to Benjamin A. Marshall by Rev. J. R. Warner, Nov 20, 1860.

Euphemia M. Knox to E. T. Rinehart by Rev. J. R. Warner, Dec 26, 1860.

Charles McLean Knox to Miss Meta R. Mason, May 12, 1864 by Jos. H. M. Mason Knox.

Elizabeth Harriet Knox to S. Johnston Rankin, March 17, 1868, by R. J. Ferguson.

Martha Virginia Knox to R. Hance Boyd, Apr 26, 1861, by J. R. Warner.

Mary Jane Rankin, dau. of Jerry was b. Sep 23, 1875.

Maria Louise Rankin, dau. of Jerry was b. June 20, 1878.

BIRTHS

Samuel Knox, b. Dec 21, 1794

Margaret Knox, b. Oct 9, 1803

Rachel Rebecca Knox, b. Apr 19, 1822

Samuel Knox, b. Oct 16, 1824

Children of John & Elizabeth K. Rankin

1. John Knox, b. Jan 14, 1827. 2. Helen Margaret Knox, b. March 11, 1829. 3. Sarah Mary Knox, b. Sep 26, 1831. 4. Euphemia Mason Knox, b.

Feb 28, 1834. 5. Charles McLean Knox, b. May 7, 1837. 6. A daughter, b. Feb 17, 1840. 7. Elizabeth Harriet, b. June 7, 1841. 8. Martha Virginia, b. Jan 26, 1844. 9. Mary Helen Rinehart, b. March 3, 1862. 10. Elizabeth Watson Rankin, b. Nov 29, 1868. 11. Baby, b. Apr 13, 1871.

DEATHS

Mrs. Rebecca Knox, d. May 28, 1843

Samuel Knox, d. May 26, 1845

Margaret Knox, d. Oct 19, 1847

A daughter d. March 7, 1840

Euphemia Mason Rinehart, d. March 10, 1862

Samuel Knox, M.D., son of Samuel, d. July 18, 1887

Even. Thomas Rinehart, d. June 1891

Samuel Johnston Rankin, d. Dec 21, 1891

Robert Hance Boyd, d. Apr 30, 1892

Helen Margaret Marshall, d. Apr 1, 1893

Charles McLean Knox, d. Feb 14, 1894

Copied by Mrs. Samuel Greenawalt, Regent, Conococheague Chapter

McCoy Family Holy Bible

National Publishing Co., Cincinnati, Ohio, 1869

MARRIAGES

Francis P. McCoy and Mary Ellen Lybarger, Sep 30, 1877

Children

1. Elsie E. McCoy to James W. Kelly, Feb 21, 1897. 2. Merit M. McCoy to Maude A. Trout, Feb 10, 1904. 3. Hugh D. McCoy to Gertrude M. Millar, March 3, 1910. 4. Hetty A. McCoy to Charles A. Ridgley, Feb 12, 1916.

BIRTHS

Francis P. McCoy, Feb 29, 1848

Mary E. McCoy, Feb 22, 1851

CHILDREN

Elsie Edna McCoy, June 24, 1878

Merit Mahlon McCoy, May 2, 1881

Hetty Ann McCoy, Sep 27, 1884

Hugh David McCoy, March 7, 1890

No deaths recorded in McCoy Bible

Telegram in McCoy Bible

"BRG 212 11 Hyndman, Penn. 26 6:10P.

  1941, Jan. 26, P.M. 6 33

  To Merit McCoy, 212 Summit Ave., Hagerstown, Md.

  John Lybarger died 2:30 today. Buried Thursday 10 A.M. Advise coming. Signed Jasper Luman.

    2:30 10 A.M. Luman"

Burials in Rest Haven Cemetery, Hagerstown, Maryland

Maude A. (Trout) McCoy, d. Oct 2, 1947

Merit Mahlon McCoy, b. May 2, 1881; d. Feb 20, 1965

Bible owned by Ellen Ardinger Zeller (Mrs. Dennis T. Zeller) National #431110, 1329 The Terrace, Hagerstown, Md. Submitted by above for Conococheague Chapter, NSDAR.

Mong Family Holy Bible

Jacob Mong, Sr., b. Apr 1757, d. Jan 26, 1815, age 57, m. Barbara Funk Mong, b. Dec 27, 1763, d. March 29, 1849, age 86.

Their Children

1. Jacob B. Mong, Feb 5, 1787 - Oct 30, 1860, age 73; m. Ann Corcoran.

Children

    a. Thomas Mong m. Louise Crawley
    Dau. Lizzie m. Ed Carner
    Daus. Helen and Bess Carney
    b. Josephine Mong m. Judge Couldran
    Children-Agnes, Annie, Angie, Jean, Tom

2. John Mong, Nov 20, 1789-Sep 20, 1863, age 73; m. Ann Rice Mong, b. 1804. Children:

    a. Susanna Mong, b. Sep 23, 1840; d. Jan 23, 1864, unmarried.
    b. Henrietta Mong, b. Sep 12, 1843; d. Aug 10, 1935, age 91; m. Jeremiah

C. Funk, b. July 27, 1841. Children

   (1) Clada Mong Funk, b. March 19, 1867; m. Frank S. Heard on Apr 21, 1896. Dau. Kathryn M., Son Robert L.

   (2) Sue Mong Funk, b. Sep 5, 1869 m. George B. Carter on Jan 12, 1892. Son Richard B. Carter, b. Apr 20, 1893.

   (3) Manie A. Funk, b. Feb 26, 1873; d. Aug 10, 1930; m. Roger T. Edmonds on Feb 27, 1896. Son-Roger T. Edmonds, Jr., b. Apr 5, 1897; Son-George H. Edmonds, b. Aug 16, 1899; Dau.-Margaret, b. Aug 24, 1906.

   (4) John Wade Funk, b. Nov 27, 1875; m. Florence Kuntz on Oct 1906; Dau.-Helen, b. June 1907; Son-John W. Jr., b. 1908.

3. Elizabeth Mong, b. Oct 20, 1791

4. George Mong, b. Jan 2, 1797, bachelor

5. Margaret Mong, b. March 5, 1799; m. John Craddock; children-Sarah Ann.

6. Mary Mong, b. July 25, 1802; m. Martin Barr, son of Col. B., Veteran of War of 1812. Children

   a. Cullin Barr m. Catherine Doub; children Ida, Mollie, Florence, Bird, William Barr.

   b. Rufus

   c. Sydenham

   d. Irene Barr m. Joe Davis; children-William, Ellen, Annie, George Davis

7. Peter Mong, b. Feb 3, 1805; d. Apr 7, 1863; m. Eliza Bauserman; children-John, George, Mollie Mong

8. Amelia Mong, b. 1809; m. John Craddock. Children

   a. Margaret Craddock m. Bucalem

   b. Ellen m. Smith

   c. John Craddock

This Bible record was submitted by Ellen Ardinger Zeller, (Mrs Dennis Zeller). The original Bible was owned by Susan Funk Carter, and was copied by her sister Manie Funk Edmonds into a small memo book. George Henry Edmonds, son of Manie Funk Edmonds, of Shillington, Penna., sent the record to Mrs. Zeller.

Nitzel Family Records

The Holy Bible, The Old and New Testaments

This bible pub. and sold by Edmund Chusing, Lunenburg, Mass. 1829

John Nitzel was b. Nov 2, 1797

Eliza Ann Nitzel was b. Apr 7, 1806

CHILDREN

William Thomas Nitzel b. June 4, 1827

Henry Clay Nitzel b. May 9, 1829

John Nitzel, III, b. Jan 22, 1831

Ann Elizabeth Nitzel b. Jan 13, 1833

Mary Susan Nitzel was born Jan 24, 1835

Eliza Nitzel b. Feb 10, 1837

James Eli Nitzel b. Oct 3, 1839

Emily Jane Nitzel b. Feb 25, 1842

William Henry Nitzel b. May 6, 1844

DEATHS

Parents: John Nitzel d. March 10, 1857

       Eliza Jan Nitzel d. Feb 2, 1888

Eliza Nitzel d. Jan 16, 1908

William Thomas Nitzel d. Sep 1, 1830

Henry Clay Nitzel d. June 30, 1831

Bible owned by Albert Preston Nitzel, 120 Linden Ave., Hagerstown, Maryland. Submitted by Ellen Ardinger Zeller (Mrs. Dennis T.), 1329 The Terrace, Hagerstown, Maryland. Conococheague Chapter, NSDAR, Hagerstown, Md.

THE NEW TESTAMENT

By: International Press, The John G. Winston Co., Philadelphia, Pennsylvania.

MARRIAGES

Albert Clifton Nitzell and Gertrude May Barlup m. Aug 15, 1900, at Hagerstown, Maryland.

Albert Clifton Nitzell, b. July 3, 1874, at Williamsport, Md.

Gertrude May Barlup, b. June 4, 1879, near Hagerstown, Md.

Albert Preston Nitzell and Dora Geneva Thomas m. Aug 20, 1927, at St. Paul's U. B. Church, Hagerstown, Md., by Rev. F. Berry Plummer.

Robert Preston Nitzell and Elizabeth Paige Logan m. June 27, 1964 at St. John's Episcopal Church, Ellicott City, Md. by Rev. E. Albert Rich.

Elizabeth Paige Logan, b. July 12, 1944

CHILDREN

Albert Preston Nitzell, b. Jan 30, 1902, Hagerstown, Md.

Dora Geneva Thomas, b. Feb 27, 1905 Sharpsburg, Md.

Robert Preston Nitzell, b. Oct 5, 1939, Hagerstown, Md.

Baptized March 17, 1940, St. Paul's U. B. Church, Hagerstown, Md. By Rev. F. Berry Plummer

DEATHS

Albert Clifton Nitzell d. Feb 19, 1940, Baltimore, Md.

Gertrude May Barlup Nitzell d. June 1, 1953, Baltimore, Md.

Bible owned by Albert Preston Nitzel, 120 Linden Ave., Hagerstown, Md. Submitted by Ellen Ardinger Zeller (Mrs. Dennis T.), 1329 The Terrace, Hagerstown, Md. Conococheague Chapter, NSDAR, Hagerstown, Md.

Bible Records - Joseph Poffenberger Family.

[See page 6 for another version of many of the same family records.]

Holy Bible - Printed by C. Alexander & Co., Philadelphia, 1834. This Bible in possession of Washington County, Historical Society, Hagerstown, Maryland.

MARRIAGES

Joseph Poffenberger was united to Mary Ann Kauffman, in the sacred bonds of Matrimony on Feb 8, 1838.

Clayton Frye was united to Susie B. Whaley, Oct 9, 1888 at Monroeville, Ohio.

Susie Frye was united in marriage to Geary A. Cooper Nov 26, 1902, at Columbus, Ohio.

Vira Frye, was united in marriage to Casper Ellsworth Kight on July 3, 1918, at Frostburg, Md.

BIRTHS

Joseph Poffenberger b. July 26, 1812

Mary Ann Kauffman b. Oct 23, 1817, Born to Casper E. Kight and Vera Frye Kight

Theodore J. Kight, Nov 2, 1919, at Keyser, West Virginia.

Casper E. Kight, Jr., Apr 8, 1926, at Piedmont, West Virginia.

George W. Frye b. Apr 19, 1898

Martha E. Frye b. Apr 7, 1842

William Clayton Frye b. Nov 19, 1863

John Ashton Nicklas b. Oct 6, 1865

Angeline Frye b. Feb 11, 1868

Catherine G???ettee, dau. of George W. and Martha E. Frye b. Dec 3, 1870, and baptized July 21, 1871, by Rev. H. J. Richardson.

DEATHS

John Ashton Michelous Frye b. Oct 6, 1865; d. March 22, 1867, aged one year, 5 months & 16 days

Martha E. Frye b. Apr 7, 1842; d. Sep 24, 1874, aged 32 years, 5 months & 17 days

George W. Fry b. Apr 12, 1838; d. Feb 19, 1872, aged 33 yrs, 8 mo, 7 days.

BIRTHS

William Clayton Frye b. Nov 19, 1863

Susie Belle Whaley b. Feb 10, 1868

Walter Clayton Frye b. July 21, 1889, son of Clayton and Susie Frye.

Isabella Martha Frye b. June 7, 1891

Vira Frye b. Aug 13, 1893

All were christened at Newark, O. Sep 11, 1893, by Rev. C. W. Gifford of the Lutheran Church

DEATHS

William Clayton Frye d. Nov 5, 1898, aged 34 yrs, 11 mo, 16 da. Departed this life at Newark, O. Buried at Monroeville, Ohio.

Susie Frye Cooper d. Feb 19, 1925, aged 57 yrs, 9 days. Departed this life at Newark, O. Buried at Monroeville, Ohio

Isabella M. Frye d. Feb 20, 1949, aged 57 yrs, 8 mo, 13 days at Keyser, W. Va. Buried at Monroeville, Ohio.

Geary A. Cooper d. Dec 22, 1951, aged 80 yrs, 11 mo, 9 days at Morgantown, W. Va. Buried at Monroeville, O.

Walter Clayton Frye d. Nov 26, 1952 at Keyser, W. Va. Buried at Monroeville, Ohio.

Legend of Bible - Found on Antietam Battlefield.

Bible was found on Antietam Battlefield by a cabinetmaker named Copper of Loudoun County, Va. Before his death gave it to his foster son William Clayton Frye, (Nov 19, 1863 - Nov 5, 1898). At age 17, W. C. Frye went to Ohio in 1880 to work for B & O R. R. At his death, it went to his daughter Vira Frye. The family then moved to W. Va., thence to Maryland.

In 1961, Mrs. Vera Frye Kight gave the Bible to her daughter-in-law, Mrs. Casper Kight as she was living in Hagerstown, near the Antietam Battlefield. Thus in 100 years it has come full circle.

Copied by Mrs. Samuel L. Greenawalt, Regent, 760 Weldon Place, Hagerstown, Maryland, for Conococheague Chapter 1963. Prepared by Mrs. Robert E. Lakin, Chairman of Genealogy for Conococheague Chapter, Hagerstown, Maryland.

Bible Records - Jacob Ridenour Family

Holy Bible - Printed by N. Y., American Bible Society, 1848

Bible in possession of Washington County Historical Society, Hagerstown, Maryland.

BIRTHS

Mary Elen Rebecca Ridenour b. Nov 11, 1850.

John Henry Ridenour b. Jan 28, 1852

Mandy Catherine Ridenour b. Sep 27, 1853

George Melanchthon Ridenour b. Feb 25, 1855

Daniel Nuton Ridenour b. Dec 18, 1856

Charles Edward Ridenour b. Aug 28, 1858

Sarah Ann Elizabeth Ridenour b. Apr 3, 1860

Emma Arbelan Ridenour b. Feb 27, 1863

DEATHS

Daniel Newton Ridenour d. Sep 19, 1857, age nine months and one day.

Lewis Macelon Ridenour d. Apr 27, 1862

Effa Jane Ridenour d. Aug 7, 1869

Etta and Effa Jane Ridenour was (sic) both born Sep 13, 1866.

BIRTHS

Susannah b. Oct 15, 1824

John b. Sep 24, 1826

William b. Oct 6, 1828

Daniel b. Feb 12, 1831

Lewis Machelon Ridenour b. Oct 5, 1861

Copied by Mrs. Samuel L. Greenawalt, Regent, 1963, for Conocacheague Chapter. Prepared by Mrs. Robert E. Lakin, Chairman of Genealogy Conocacheague Chapter, Hagerstown, Maryland.

Jacob Ridenour b. March 8, 1828

Susanna Ridenour b. Oct 15, 1824

"Amelia Welty's Book, Sep 2, 1825."

Holy Bible; Pub. by C. Ewer & T. Bedington: Boston, 1827

MARRIAGES

Michael Welty m. Amelia South, Aug 22, 1839

BIRTHS

Daniel Welty b. May 25, 1840

William Geary Welty b. June 26, 1841

Rakel Ann Welty b. July 1, 1843

Sarow Elen Welty b. June 21, 1846

Martin L. Welty b. Aug 22, 1850

William Alforde Welty b. Oct 8, 1853

Michael Welty b. Sep 27, 1814

Amelia Welty b. Apr 10, 1816

DEATHS

Michael Welty d. Oct 27, 1889; aged 75 yrs. and 27 days

Martin Luther Welty d. March 29, 1896; aged 45 yrs, 7 mo, 7 da

Amelia Welty d. Oct 27, 1867; aged 51 yrs, 6 mo, 17 da.

William Alfred Welty d. Jan 25, 1920; aged 66 yr, 3 mo, 17 da.

Holy Bible
Thomas, Cowperthwait & Co., 1850

MARRIAGES

Nov 22, 1849, Rufus H. Wilson, of Washington Co., Md. to Elizabeth Brewer, of Franklin Co., Md.(sic)--should be Pa.

June 29, 1876 John H. Wilson, of Washington Co., Md. to Margaretta Ozella Huyett, of Washington Co., Md.

Dec 25, 1899 Clyde Huyett Wilson of Washington Co., Md. to Mary Anders Adams of Washington Co., Md.

Apr 12, 1911 Margaretta Helen Wilson of Washington Co., Md. to Edgar Thomas Hayman of Anne Arundel Co., Md. b. in Worcester Co., Md.

Apr 30, 1923 Mary Adams Wilson of Washington Co., Md. to Maurice Hepburn Jones of Kent Co. - 4th son

Jan 27, 1940 Mary Wilson Jones of Washington Co., Md. to Addison Barnwell Cooke

BIRTHS

Rufus H. Wilson, Sr. b. Feb 18, 1815, in Calvert Co., Md

Elizabeth Wilson b. Nov 25, 1825, in Franklin Co., Pa.

John Hamilton Wilson b. Aug 31, 1850 in Washington Co., Md.

Mary Elizabeth Wilson b. Oct 19, 1851, in Washington Co., Md.

Rufus Hillary Wilson, Jr. b. March 21, 1853, in Washington Co., Md.

Margaretta O. Huyett, dau. of Daniel & Margaretta Brinham Huyett, b. Jan 2, 1858, in Washington Co., Md.; d. July 3, 1936.

BIRTHS

Clyde Huyett Wilson, son of John H. & Margaretta O. Wilson, b. July 12, 1878, in Washington Co., Md.

Mary Anders Adams, dau. of John U. & Elizabeth Adams b. Aug 2, 1877, in Washington Co., Md.

Margaretta Helen Wilson, dau. of John H. and Margaretta O. Wilson, b. July 4, 1899, in Washington Co., Md.

Edgar Thomas Hayman, son of Elijah R. and Margaret Payne Hayman, b. Oct 19, 1885, in Worcester Co. (Maryland)

Mary Adams Wilson, dau. of Clyde H. & Mary A. Wilson, b. Aug 2, 1900, in Washington Co., Md.

Maurice Hepburn Jones, son of Harrison Piper and Minnie A. Jones, b. Apr 22, 1896, Kent Co., Md.

Addison Barnwell Cooke, son of J. Addison Cooke and Mary Sams Cooke, b. Dec 10, 1902, in Baltimore, Md.

Mary Wilson Cooke b. at Wilson's, Washington Co., Md. Buried in St. Paul's Cemetery on old Route 40, Washington Co., Md. Departed this life June 26, 1966. The entire family buried on same lot of Rufus H. Wilson.

Mary Wilson Cooke-first husband was Maurice Hepburn Jones; second husband was Addison Barnwell Cooke

DEATHS

Mary Elizabeth Wilson d. Feb 3, 1854, aged 2 yr., 3 mo. 14 da.

Rufus Hillery Wilson, Jr. d. Sep 25, 1854 aged 1 yr, 6 mo., 4 da.

Elizabeth Wilson d. Dec 1, 1854 aged 29 yr., 6 da.

Rufus Hillery Wilson, son of Lancelot Wilson, Jr. and Harriet Hillery Wilson of Calvert Co., Md. d. Nov 25, 1882, 67 yr., 9 mo., 7 da.

John Hamilton Wilson, son of Rufus Hillery Wilson and Elizabeth Brewer Wilson, d. May 6, 1924, aged 73 yr., 8 mo., 6 da.

DEATHS

Margaretta O. Wilson, wife of John H. Wilson, d. July 3, 1936, aged 78 yr., 6 mo., 1 da.

Mary Adams Wilson d. Jan 6, 1933, 56 yr., 5 mo., 4 da.

Clyde Huyett Wilson d. Jan 6, 1950, 71 yr., 5 mo., 25 da.

Addison Barnwell Cooke, husband of Mary A. Wilson, d. Aug. 12, 1958, aged 55 yr., 8 mo., 2 da.

Edgar Thomas Hayman, son of Elijah Robert Hayman and Margaret Payne Hayman, d. Jan 12, 1963

MARRIAGES

John Brewer m. Elizabeth Fiery

Rufus Wilson m. dau. Elizabeth Brewer

James R. E. Brewer (cousin of John H. Wilson) d. July 6, 1936. Died at the wheel of his car between house and store at Wilson's.

Lawrence or Lancelot Wilson, Jr. m. Harriet Hillary Calvert Co., Md. Prince George Co., Md. (1815), parents of Rufus Hillery Wilson

Dr. S. W. Owen of St. John's Lutheran Church, Hagerstown, Md. m. John H. Wilson and Margaretta Huyett, 1876. Also m. E. T. Hayman and Margaretta Wilson, 1911.

David Benjamin Franklin Sanders (colored), Washington Co., Md. d. June 1939, aged 74 yrs. Faithful servant with Wilson family 56 years.

John Hanna, Revolutionary War -L

    National #316486 (Ser. 4, Vol 70)

    Dau. Mary m. John Brinham

    Dau. Margaretta m. Daniel Huyett

    Dau. Margaretta m. John Wilson

Dau. Margaretta m. Edgar Hayman

Henry Hillary, Prince George Co., Md.; Rev. Soldier

Sons, George and Thomas; Daughter Harriet m. Lawrence Wilson.
Bible in possession of Mrs. Hayman of Wilson's, Md. Copied for Conococheague Chapter, NSDAR, Hagerstown, Md. by Mrs. Samuel L. Greenawalt.

Wolfkill Bible

The Cottage Bible, Published by Case, Lockwood & Co., Harford 1859

BIRTHS

Jacob Wolfkill b. Oct 22, 1825

Jane Brinham, wife of Jacob Wolfkill, b. Dec 21, 1823

Brinham Wolfkill b. Apr 29, 1850

Melvin Perry Wolfkill b. Sep 12, 1851

Mary Jane Wolfkill b. Sep 5, 1853

Lilly Anna Wolfkill b. March 5, 1855

Virginia America Wolfkill b. Dec 9, 1856

Jacob Calvin Wolfkill b. Apr 21, 1859

John Ellsworth Wolfkill b. July 4, 1865

MARRIAGES

Jacob Wolfkill and Jane Brinham m. Dec 14, 1848

Perry Beckley and Virginia Wolfkill m. Aug 20, 1874

DEATHS

Melvin Perry Wolfkill d. Apr 6, 1856

John Ellsworth Wolfkill d. July 14, 1865

Jacob Calvin Wolfkill d. Oct 23, 1880, aged 21. 6 mos. 2 da.

Jacob Wolfkill d. March 2, 1884, aged 58, 4, 10 da.

Jane Brinham Wolfkill d. Dec 21, 1915, aged 92 yr.

Bible in possession of Helen Hershey Miller (Mrs. Russell Miller) 147 N. Artizan St., Williamsport, Md. Submitted by Ellen Ardinger Zeller (Mrs. Dennis T. Zeller) National #431110, 1329 The Terrace, Hagerstown, Md.

Copied for Conococheague Chapter, NSDAR, Hagerstown, Md. by Mrs. Samuel L. Greenawalt, Librarian, Conococheague Chapter.

Wilmore's Analytical Reference Bible, edited by Philip Schaff; J. A. Wilmore & Co., New York, 1900. Family Bible in possession of Richard Doub, Rt. 2, Williamsport, Md.

GREAT GRAND PARENTS:

Jacob Wolfkill, b. Oct. 22, 1825, Beaver Creek, Md.; d. March 2, 1884, Huyetts, Md.

Jane Wolfkill, b. Dec 21, 1823, Beaver Creek, Md.; d. Dec 21, 1915, Hagerstown, Md.

GRAND PARENTS

Richard Perry W. Beckley, b. Apr 16, 1855, Hagerstown, Md.; d. Dec 29, 1937, Hagerstown, Md.

Virginia A. (Wolfkill) Beckley, b. Dec 9, 1856, Hagerstown, Md.; d. July 10, 1921, Halfway, Md.

They were m. Aug 20, 1874, Baltimore, Md.

PARENTS

Elmer R. Beckley, b. Oct 28, 1881, Centreville, Md.; d. Oct 3, 1923, Halfway, Md., m. Vernie Kendle, b. March 10, 1886, Huyetts, Md.; d. Nov 9, 1957.

Copied from a notarized copy, notarized by Merle Kenneth Hoover for Ida Mae (Beckley) Lehman, Oct 20, 1967. Submitted by Ellen Ardinger Zeller (Mrs. Dennis T. Zeller), National #431110. Copied for Conococheague Chapter, NSDAR, Hagerstown, Md. by Mrs. Samuel L. Greenawalt, Chapter Librarian.

Family Bible of Mr. & Mrs. Edward C. Doub

Bible in possession of Richard Doub, Rt.2, Williamsport, Md.

PARENTS

Richard Perry W. Beckley, b. Apr 16, 1855, Hagerstown, Md; d. Dec 29, 1937

Virginia America Beckley, b. Dec 9, 1856, Hagerstown, Md.; d. July 10, 1921; m. Aug 20, 1874, Baltimore, Md.

CHILDREN

1. Abner Doub, b. Feb 1865, Beaver Creek, Md.; m. 1888 to Susanna Stockslager

2. William D. Doub, b. Jan 14, 1867, Beaver Creek, Md.; m. Oct 1895 to Ida E. Garling

3. Mollie R. Doub, b. Dec 23, 1868, Beaver Creek, Md.; m. Jan 1891 to Abner Barnhart

4. Jennie F. Doub, b. June 25, 1871, Beaver Creek, Md.; d. Oct 17, 1896

5. Edward C. Doub, b. July 14, 1873, Beaver Creek, Md.,; d. Sep 28, 1948; m. L. Grace Beckley, Aug 25, 1903

6. Daisy D. Doub, b. Dec 22, 1874, Beaver Creek,; d. Dec 25, 1951; m. Dec 22, 1903 Charles Sprecker

7. Catharine Doub, b. Oct 22, 1876, Beaver Creek

8. Harry G. Doub, b. Apr 28, 1882, Hagerstown, Md.; m. Sep 1908 to Delva Bowers

9. Charles Doud [sic], b. Apr 28, 1882, Hagerstown, Md.

10. L. Grace Beckley, b. Sep 22, 1876, Hagerstown, Md.; d. Dec 16, 1940; m. Aug 25, 1903 to Edward C. Doub

11. Elmer R. Beckley, b. Oct 28, 1881, Centreville, Md.; d. Oct 3, 1923; m. Dec 9, 1908 to Vernie Kendle

12. M. Guy Beckley, b. May 27, 1887, Centreville, Md.; m. Apr 1909 Nancy Knode

13. D. Ernest Beckley, b. Aug 19, 1891, Centreville, Md.; d. June 10, 1945; m. March 1, 19ll to Amelia Knode

Beckley, Wolfkill Tombstones, Rose Hill Cemetery, Hagerstown, Md.

Elmer R. Beckley, b. Oct 28, 1881; d. Oct 3, 1923. His wife, Vernie E. Beckley, b. March 10, 1886; d. Nov 9, 1957. Buried on lot of John M. Kendle-Kendal, Lot #15, Section 1, Range E.

Richard P. Beckley (father of Elmer R. Beckley), b. Apr 16, 1855; d. Dec 29, 1937. His wife, Virginia A. Wolfkill, b. Dec 9, 1856; d. July 10, 1921. Buried on Lot 76, north half section 14, Range B.

Jacob Wolfkill, b. Oct 22, 1825; d. March 2, 1883. His wife, Jane Wolfkill, b. Dec 21, 1823; d. Dec 21, 1915. Buried Lot 66, Section 1.

Copied from a notarized copy, notary M. Kenneth Hoover, for Ida Mae (Beckley) Lehman. Submitted by Ellen Ardinger Zeller (Mrs. Dennis T. Zeller). National #431110. Copied for Conococheague Chapter, NSDAR, Hagerstown, Md. by Mrs. Samuel L. Greenawalt, 1967.

Zeller Family Bible

Daniel Edward Zeller, b. Jan 2, 1852, near Cearfoss, Md.; d. Oct 20, 1923, Broadfording, Md.; m. Dec 22, 1875, Hagerstown, Md. to Mary Louise Cunningham, b. June 24, 1852, near Cearfoss, Md.; d. March 17, 1941, near Cearfoss, Md.

CHILDREN

Bruce Henry Zeller, b. Oct 10, 1876, residence Hagerstown, Md.; d. June 7, 1952; m. Bertie Mae Barr. Both buried Salem Cemetery, Cearfoss, Md.

Charles Garfield Zeller, b. Nov 3, 1880, Hagerstown, Md.; d. Nov 27, 1962, buried Salem Cemetery; m. Ethel Kohr (living 2/8/1968) Thurmont, Md.

Rachel E. Zeller, b. Apr 18, 1885, Hagerstown, Md.; d. Dec 13, 1937; buried Salem Cemetery, Cearfoss, Md.; m. James L. Stouffer, b. Aug 5, 1887, Washington Co., Md.; living 2/8/1968, Glen Echo, Washington, D.C.

Dennis Tobias Zeller, b. Oct 18, 1890, near Cearfoss, Md., living Hagerstown, Md. 2/8/1968; m. Dec 22, 1941, Winchester, Va. by Rev. Carl Honeycutt, Lutheran to Ellen Betty Ardinger.

Submitted by Ellen Ardinger Zeller (Mrs. Dennis T. Zeller), 1329 The Terrace, Hagerstown, Md. DAR National #431110

Dennis T. Zeller, SAR, National #95269, SAR, MD State, #1895

Copied for Conococheague Chapter, NSDAR, Hagerstown, Md. by Mrs. Samuel L. Greenawalt, Librarian and Chairman of Genealogical Records, 1968.

CATHARINE MULLENDORE'S BIBLE.

"New Illustrated Devotional and Practical Polygot Family Biele," published by the National Publishing Co., Ziegler & McCurdy, Jones Brothers & Co.

Entered according to Act of Congress in the year 1870 by J. R. Jones, In the Office of the Librarian of Congress at Washington, District of Columbia.

This certifies that the Rite of Holy Matrimony was celebrated between Jacob Mullendore of Washington County, Md. and Catharine Blecher of Washington County, Md. on April 13th, 1823 at John Blecher's by George A. Guething. Witnesses: Eli Crampton, Elizabeth Hill

Marriages

Jacob Mullendore m. Apr 13, 1823.

Catharine Mullendore m. Apr 13, 1823.

Mahala Mullendore m. March 7, 1844.

Malinda J. Mullendore m. Dec 14, 1843.

John A. Mullendore m. Dec 4, 1862.

Daniel M. Mullendore m. Oct 15, 1853.

Jacob H. Mullendore m. Nov 12, 1850.

Josiah E. Mullendore m. Apr 1871.

Julia A. Mullendore m. Sep 14, 1876.

Martha A. Mullendore m. March 16, 1865.

Births

Jacob Mullendore b. Feb 10, 1795; d. Aug 17, 1854 aged 59 yrs. 6 mos. 7 das.

Catherine Mullendore b. March 4, 1806, d. Jan 8, 1876 aged 69 yrs. 10 mos. 2 das.

Mahala A. Mullendore b. June 7, 1824; d. Feb 13, 1845 aged 20 yrs. 8 mos. 6 das.

Malinda J. Mullendore b. Nov 30, 1825; d. Apr 12, 1887 aged 61 yrs. 4 mos. 12 das.

John A. Mullendore b. Aug 28, 1827; d. Apr 19, 1897 aged 69 yrs 7 mos. 21 das.

Daniel M. Mullendore b. Oct 3, 1829; d. Nov 7, 1912 aged 83 yrs

Jacob H. Mullendore b. Nov 17, 1831; d. Sep 4, 1898 aged 66 yrs 10 mos 17 das.

Josiah E. Mullendore b. Sep 12, 1833; d. Sep 21, 1888 aged 55 yrs 9 das.

Mary C. Mullendore b. Apr 26, 1838; d. Mar 9, 1839 aged 10 mos 11 das

Julia A. E. Mullendore b. Apr 26, 1838.

Martha A. Mullendore b. Sep 10, 1841.

Henry H. Ross Bible

Henry Harrison Ross and Sarah Hause m. at Waynesboro 22 Oct 1867 in presence of Mrs. A. Buhrman by Rev. A. Buhrman at the Lutheran Parsonage.

Marriages

George W. Ross and Laura A. Moore, Dec 2, 1896.

Effie Myrtle Ross and Walter B. Sleasman, Dec 23, 1896.

Charles Ross and Alice L. Sleasman, May 8, 1907.

Daisy Ann Ross and John W. Snyder, June 4, 1914.

Births

Henry H. Ross b. March 10, 1842.

Sarah Ross b. Jan 20, 1842.

George Washington Ross, first son of Henry H. and Sarah Ross b. Sep 11, 1868.

Lilah Cathryn Ross, first dau. of Henry H. and Sarah Ross b. June 28, 1871.

Effie Myrtle Ross, second dau. of Henry H. and Sarah Ross b. Sep 11, 1874.

Daisy Ann Ross, third dau. of Henry H. and Sarah Ross, b. Sep 9, 1876.

Charlie Ross, second son of Henry H. and Sarah Ross b. Nov 18, 1880.

Deaths

Henry Harrison Ross d. Oct 4, 1914

Sarah Ross d. March 7, 1921

George W. Ross d. Feb 7, 1942

Laura A. Ross d. Feb 29, 1948

Charlie Ross d. Feb 23, 1956

Lilah C. Ross d. Oct 15, 1960

Walter B. Sleasman d. Nov 7, 1959

Effie M. Sleasman d. Sep 13, 1962

Daisy A. Snyder d. June 20, 1963

Information copied from Ingram Family Bible, provided by Huyette B. Oswald

Edward Ingram b. Jan 6, 1812

Martha Ann Huyett, wife of Edward Ingram, b. Mar 1, 1824

    Mary Eliza Ingram b. Aug 24, 1846

    Elizabeth Florence Ingram b. Dec 1, 1847

    Laura Virginia Ingram b. July 1, 1850

    Rachel Catherine Ingram b. Dec 7, 1853

    Martha Ellen Ingram b. Feb 16, 1853

    Edith Huyett Ingram b. Nov 1, 1860

Daniel Huyett d. May 14, 1869, age 82 years 11 months 4 days

Edward Ingram d. Mar 2, 1883, age 71 years 2 months 14 days

Martha Ann Ingram d. Mar 30, 1883, age 59 years and 29 days

Aaron Funk Rohrer, husband of Edith Rohrer, d. Mar 4, 1933, age 75 years 8 months, 7 days

Edith H. I. Rohrer, wife of Aaron Funk Rohrer, d. June 23, 1944 age 84 years 4 months 8 days

Martha E. Ingram d. Sep 1, 1872, age 17 years 6 months 16 days

Laura Ingram d. Oct 27, 1901, age 51 years 2 months 26 days

Martha E. Ingram d. Aug 2, 1903, age 56 years 11 months 10 days

Elizabeth I. Oswald d. July 12, 1907, age 59 years 7 months 10 days

Rachel Catharine Ingram d. Mar 29, 1926, age 73 years 1 month 22 days

Edith Huyett Ingram confirmed at Cavetown German Reformed Church May 23, 1874

Mary E. Ingram confirmed at same church May 26, 1865

Aaron F. Rohrer confirmed at same church Oct 10, 1896

Rachel Catharine Ingram confirmed same church May 13, 1871

Edith Huyett Ingram confirmed at same church May 23, 1874

Ludwig Huyett married Potter, had children: 1. Jacob; 2. Daniel; 3. Margaret Hogmire; 4. Elizabeth Tritle; 5. Mary Knode

Catherine Ingram m. William Huyett--buried at Cavetown--had no children

Cynthia Ingram m. Amos Price--had children: 1. Mahlon; 2. William; 3. Rachael; 4. Catharine

William Ingram m. Sarah Wagner of the West--had children: 1. Henrietta; 2. Mary; 3. John; 4. Tilly; 5. Jennie

Daniel Huyett (of Ludwig) m. (1) Mary Swope, (2) Martha Gaither. Children of 1st wife: Peter; 2. Eliza; 3. Samuel; 4. William; 5. Henry; 6. Martha Huyett Ingram. Children of 2nd wife: 1. Henrietta; 2. Daniel G.

Sarah Ingram, an old maid, buried at Beaver Creek

Rachel Ingram, buried at Beaver Creek

Susan Ingram m. Samuel Swope--had children: 1. Ingram; 2. Peter; 3. Laretta; 4. Elizabeth; 5. Cecelia

Elizabeth (Betsy) Tritle m. Jacob Tritle--had children: 1. Jacob; 2. Lewis; 3. Lewis; 4. Margaret Sangaree; 5. Lizzie Tritle

Mary (Polly) Knode m. Henry Knode--had children: 1. Joseph; 2. Lewis; 3. Daniel

Margaretta (Peggy) Hogmire m. Daniel Hogmire--had children: 1. Daniel Hogmire

John Huyett (of Ludwig) m. Grove--had children: 1. John; 2. William; 3. Joseph; 4. Lewis; 5. Susan; 6. Fannie, m. Benjain Beck (grandparents of Huyette B. Oswald)

Jacob Huyett (of Ludwig)--had children: 1. Ellen; 2. Joseph (died age 2); 3. Bennie; 4. Elizabeth Huyett Beard; 5. Cynthia; 6. Edward

"My grandfather Joseph Ingram m. Rachel Perrin"--had children: 1. Elizabeth; 2. John; 3. Susan; 4. Sarah; 5. Benjamin; 6. Joseph (d. age 2); 7. Edward; 8. William; 9. Catharine; 10. Rachel (single)

Poffenberger Bible

MARRIAGES

Joseph Poffenberger m. Mary Ann Kauffman, Feb 8, 1838

Clayton Frye m. Susie B. Whaley, Oct 9, 1888 at Monroeville, Ohio

Susie Frye m. Geary A. Cooper, Nov 26, 1902 at Columbus, Ohio

Vira Frye m. Casper Ellsworth Kight July 3, 1918 at Frostburg, Md.

BIRTHS

Jos. Poffenberger b. July 26, 1812

Mary Ann Kauffman b. Oct 23, 1817

Born to Casper E. Kight and Vira Frye Kight: Theodore J. Kight, Nov 2, 1919 at Keyser, W.Va. and Casper E. Kight, Jr., b. April 8, 1926 at Piedmont, W.Va.

George W. Frye b. April 19, 1898

Martha E. Frye b. April 7, 1842

William Clayton Frye b. Nov 19, 1863

John Ashton Nichles b. Oct 6, 1865

Angeline Frye b. Feb 11, 1868

Catharine Germettee, dau. of Geo. W. and Martha E. Frye b. Dec 3, 1870, bap. July 21, 1871 by Rev. H. J. Richardson

William Clayton Frye d. Nov 5, 1898 aged 34 years, 11 months, 16 days at Newark, Ohio, buried at Monroeville, Ohio

Susie Belle Whaley b. Feb 10, 1868

Walter Clayton Frye b. July 21, 1889, son of Clayton and Susie Frye

Isabella Martha Frye b. June 7, 1891

Vira Frye b. Aug 13, 1893

All were christened at Newark, Ohio Sep 11, 1893 by Rev. C. W. Gifford of the Lutheran Church

DEATHS

John Ashton Mechelous Frye b. Oct 6, 1865; d. Mar 22, 1867, aged one year, 5 months and 16 days

Martha E. Fry b. April 7, 1842; d. Sep 24, 1874, aged 32 years, 5 months, 17 days

George W. Fry b. April 12, 1838; d. Feb 19, 1872, aged 33 years, 8 months, 7 days

Susie Frye Cooper d. Feb 19, 1925, aged 57 years, 9 days at Newark Ohio, buried at Monroeville, Ohio

Isabella M. Frye d. Feb 20, 1949 aged 57 yrs, 8 mo, 13 days at Keyser, W. VA, buried at Monroeville, Ohio

Geary A. Cooper d. Dec 22, 1951, aged 80 years, 11 months, 9 days at Morgantown, W.Va. Buried at Monroeville, Ohio

Walter Clayton Frye d. Nov 26, 1952 at Keyser, W. Va., buried at Monroeville, Ohio

Windsor Family Bible

Newman Windsor b. Dec 20, 1789

Fanny Windsor b. Aug 29, 1790

Richard L. Windsor b. Jan 8, 1816

Robert N. Windsor b. May 4, 1818

Elizabeth F. Windsor b. March 15, 1820

Joseph R. Windsor b. Dec 19, 1821

John H. Windsor b. Aug 5, 1824

Emily C. Windsor b. June 1, 1827

Edw. Windsor Mealey b. Aug 23, 1846

Joseph Albert Mealey b. Sep 24, 1848

Richard Clinton Mealey b. June 17, 1850

Frederick Lawson Mealey b. Mar 12, 1852

DEATHS

Fanny Windsor d. Dec 21, 1828

John H. Windsor d. Sep 1824

Newman Windsor d. Mar 29, 1830

Joseph P. Windsor d. Dec 25, 1835

Elizabeth Frances (Windsor) Mealey d. July 2, 1891

Edward Windsor Mealey d. Apr 28, 1911

Joseph Albert Mealey d. Apr 13, 1854

Richard Clinton Mealey d. Apr 26, 1854

Frederick Lawson Mealey d. Mar 25, 1856

Edward Merryman Mealey, husband of Elizabeth Frances (Windsor) Mealey d. May 26, 1871

Laura Gertrude (Parks) Mealey d. Sep 20, 1897

BIRTHS

Hannah b. Mar 10, 1794

Jesse b. Mar 27, 1796

Jordan b. Aug 29, 1804

Agness b. Jan 8, 1806

Ralph b. Dec 20, 1809

Frielin b. Nov 12, 1810

Mary b. Feb 10, 1814

Lindy b. May 20, 1814

Jiles b. July 17, 1817

Jenny b. Mar 12, 1819

Ritter b. Apr 29, 1820

George b. June 20, 1822

Ephraim b. Oct 7, 1824

Lewis b. Feb 18, 1827

Ely b. Nov 25, 1828

Lisa b. Mar 31, 1830

MARRIAGES

Newman Windsor m. Fanny Windsor Aug 12, 1813

Edw. M. Mealey m. Elizabeth Frances Windsor Nov 11, 1841

Edward Windsor Mealey m. Laura Gertrude Parks June 1, 1876

Edward Windsor Mealey m. Adelaide Bessy Allderdice Oct 15, 1895

Boyer Family Record

Wilkin Boyer m. Ann Maria Phesant Sep 21, 1837

Wilkin Boyer b. Sep 27, 1815

Ann Maria Boyer b. Feb 25, 1816

David Boyer b. Nov 3, 1839

Wilkin Boyer d. Nov 10, 1900 aged 84 years 1 month 13 days

Ann Maria Boyer d. Sunday, Feb 11, 1906 aged 89 years, 11 months, 16 days.

Speck Family Record

John M. Walker m. Eliza Pousal(?) Dec 16, 1828

Martin Specks m. Nancy Spickler Oct 16, 1810

David Anderson m. Mary Speck Sep 13, 1836

John Hicks m. Elizabeth Speck Jan 28, 1840

David Speck m. Rebecca Stouffer Dec 28, 1843

Martin Speck m. Isabella Pittenger Feb 8, 1844

Catharine Speck m. Daniel Middlekauff Mar 12, 1861

Margaret ??? m. Jos. A. Hershey Mar 24, 1863

Samuel Speck m. Elizabeh Jacobs Apr 21, 1863

BIRTHS

John M. Walker b. Jan 11, 1805

Eliza Walker b. Nov 22, 1810

Margareta E. Walker b. Nov 6, 1829

John P. Walker b. Feb 14, 1831

Martin Speck, Sen. b. Nov 15, 1789

Nancy Speck b. July 24, 1790

Mary Speck b. Apr 15, 1811

Elizabeth Speck b. Aug 28, 1812

Susannah Speck b. Jan 20, 1815

Martin Speck b. Jan 3, 1817

Frederick Speck b. Dec 12, 1818

DEATHS

John P. Walker d. Apr 9, 1831 aged one month, 3 weeks, one day

Susannah Speck d. Nov 20, 1824 aged 10 years, 10 months

Martin Speck, Sr. d Mar 24, 1852 aged 62 years, 4 months, 9 days

Ann Speck d. Oct 21, 1858 aged 68 years, two months 28 days

DEATHS

Martin Speck d. Apr 11, 1877

Isabella Speck d. Jan 2, 1878

Polly Speck d. Dec 22, 1892 at her home in Tiffen, Ohio

Peter Speck d. at his home in Tiffen, Ohio Jan 9, 1896, age 72 yrs

Elizabeth Hick d. Oct 15, 1898 at home Broadfording, aged 86 yrs, 1 mo, 17 days

David Speck d. June 19, 1900 at his home near Ceafoss, age 77

Mrs. Mary Anderson d. Feb 1, 1900 at home at Hedgunville, WVa, age 89 yrs, 10 mos, 1 day

Mrs. Catherine Flook d. Dec 7, 1902 at home

Mrs. Nannie Meyer d. Apr 6, 1903 in Matamoras, Ohio

BIRTHS

Catharine Speck was b. Feb 1, 1821

David Speck was b. Apr 5, 1823

Peter Speck was b. Jan 11, 1825

Nancy Speck was b. Feb 8, 1827

Samuel Speck was b. June 3, 1829

Margaret Speck was b. July 6, 1832

Family Bible of William John Besler bap. on Easter Sunday, Mar 23, 1895 in the Chapel of the College of St. James, Washington Co., Md.

by John B. Kerfoot

Mother b. in Witinburg near Stutgard 1819, came to America in the year 1840 & married in 1843

[Can't read the rest of this record.]

The Jones Bible presented to Charles Howard Beck by his Grandmother Jones March 28, 1870 in presence of his father & cousin Elizabeth Bovey

Jonathan Jones m. (1) Aug 1, 1826 Elizabeth Resh, both of Washington County, Maryland

Jonathan Jones m. (2) Apr 14, 1833 Elizabeth Bovey of Washington County, Maryland. She was b. Feb 22, 1800

Jonathan Jones b. Oct 28, 1794; wife Elizabeth Jones b. Jan 27, 1797

David Washington Jones b. May 8, 1827, son of Jonathan & Elizabeth

Dau. Maryann Jones b. June 1, 1829

Son Daniel Martin Jones b. Apr 11, 1832

By the second wife:

Dau. Sophia Rosan Jones b. Jul 10, 1834

Sons Simon & Jacob Bovey Jones, two twins were b. Oct 28, 1836

Son William Bovey Jones b. Feb 1, 1839

DEATHS

Daniel Martin Jones d. Sep 26, 1832 aged 5 mos 15 days

Simon Jones d. Nov 6, 1836 aged 10 days

Jacob Bovey Jones d. Dec 24, 1836 aged 1 month, 26 days

William Bovey Jones d. Aug 4, 1858 aged 19 yrs, 6 month and 4 days And Expressed a good hope of getting to heaven and no fears to die

"Oh if my lord would come to meet

My soul would stretch her wings in haste

Fly Fearless through death's Iron Gate,

Nor feel the sorrows as She Passed."

Elizabeth Jones d. Apr 23, 1832 in hope of Glorious Imortality. Last words: "Glory, Glory." Aged 35 yrs, 2 mos, 26 d.

Jonathan Jones d. Oct 2, 1867 in hope of a Glorious Immortality, aged 72 years, 11 mos. & 5 days

Elizabeth Jones* d. July 13, 1870 aged 70 yrs. 4 mos. & 20 days. Buried in the United Brethren Graveyard, Hagerstown, Md.

*This name is marked with yellow highliner pen as are all the other names which indicate Elizabeth Bovey Jones' relations on the copy of the bible, so it would indicate that this is Elizabeth Bovey Jones.

Storm Family Bible

Presented to Katie C. Storm by F. E. Storm Feb 3, 1890

Frank E. Storm of Boonsboro, Md. m. Katie C. Falconer of Boonsboro, Md. Apr 13, 1881 at John Murdock in the presence of Geo. H. Beckley, Boonsboro

BIRTHS

Hattie Storm b. Mar 10, 1882
Allice C. Storm b. Aug 5, 1883
Pauline S. Storm b. Mar 31, 1888
John F. Storm b. Jan 20, 1890
Harriet C. Storm b. June 30, 1892
Frances M. Storm b. Apr 16, 1894

DEATHS

Hattie Storm d. Sep 17, 1882

Murdock Family Bible

Presented to Mrs. H. C. Murdock by her husband John Murdock

Newspaper clipping: "John Murdock died at Boonsboro Saturday noon, after a short illness, of heart failure and general debility, in his 77th year.

Mr. Murdock was a native of Ireland and came to this country when quite a young man. He married Miss Harriett Barber, of New Market, Frederick county, who survives him. Mr. Murdock, for a number of years prior to the war, was supervisor of a section of the National turnpike in Fredrick County. In the fifties he came to Washington county and has since resided in Boonsboro district [--- long description of his character ---] He represented this county in the Maryland Legislature in the session of 1868; was magistrate of Boonsboro district from 1869 until May 1, 1896, save an interregnum of one term of two years, served as president of the Boonsboro Cemetery Association for 28 years. Burgess of Boonsboro for one term, and has filled all the official positions incident to membership in the council of the Lutheran church of which we was a consistent member.

He and the late Gov. Hamilton were warm and consistant friends and maintained intimate relations many years, each holding in high regard in the other the sterling qualities that characterized them both.

The funeral services will be held at his late residence Monday afternoon at 4 o'clock. Interment in the cemetery at Boonsboro. "

This is an obituary notice from a newspaper clipping. Next to it handwritten is this: "Dide May 23, 1896" also the bible verse Numbers 23, Chapt. 10.

John Murdock of Frederick County m. Harriet C. Barbour of Frederick County Sep 23, 1844 at Newmarkett by Rev. Margan [?]

Frances E. Storm m. Katie C. Falconer Apr --, 1881

BIRTHS

Hattie Storm b. Mar 10, 1882

John Murdock b. Aug the (blank)

Harriet C. Barbour b. Aug 13, 1823

Clementine E. Barbour b. Aug 16, 1831

Oliver L. Falconer b. Oct 10, 1831

Lucian E. Falconer b. Aug 5, 1853

Clemintine L. K. Falconer b. Dec 20, 1855

Caroline M. Barbour b. Jul 7, 1825

Achsah A. Barbour b. Jan 5, 1835

DEATHS

Hattie Storm d. Sep 17, 1882, aged six months and seven days

Catharine Barbour d. Sep 20, 1853

Jonsy Barbour d. --- 1869

"Records copied from Family Bibles of Washington County, Maryland - Property of Rachael S. Schwartz, 1014 Hamilton Blvd., Hagerstown, Md." [These records are handwritten in a notebook.]

From Bible of J. Forney Young, Long Meadow

William S. Young and Mary A. Hilt m. by Rev. S. M. Templeton in Middletown, Butler Co., Ohio, Dec 6, 1847

William S. Young and Emelia Forney m. at Hanover, Pa. by Rev. W. K. Gieber June 29, 1870

George Young, second son of Wm. S. and Mary Hilt Young, m. Mar 1884 to Lizzie R. Forney, dau. of Jacob Forney of Hanover, Pa.

Jacob Forney Young, second son of William Sholl Young and Emelia Forney Young m. Sep 23, 1908 to Temperance Eliza Butler of Stillwater, Minnesota.

William Piatt Young, first son of Jacob Forney Young and Temperance Butler Young, m. May 16, 1936 at Aquina P. E. Church at Stafford, Va. by Rev. Henry Heaton, to Margaret Anne Moore of Aldie, Va.

Temperance Glenn Butler Young, dau. of Jacob Forney Young and Temperance Butler Young, m. Oct 26, 1937 to William Charles Conley, Jr. of Hagerstown, Md. at Long Meadows Farm, Washington Co., Md. by Rev. Scott R. Wagner.

Jacob Forney Young, Jr. second son of Jacob Forney Young and Temperance Butler Young m. May 21, 1942 at Presbyterian Church, Hagerstown, Md. to Hannah Driscoll Kingston of Hagerstown, Md. by Rev. G. Audrey Young.

BIRTHS

William S. Young b. Hanover, York Co., Pa. Dec 25, 1825

Mary A. Hilt b. in East Berlin, Adams Co., Pa. Jan 24, 1830

Charles Young b. in Middletown, Butler Co., Ohio, Sep 20, 1848

George Young b. in Middletown, Butler Co., Ohio, May 27, 1853

Grace Young b. in Baltimore, Md. on Jan 29, 1863

Emelia Forney b. in Hanover, York Co., Pa., July 14, 1841

Wm. Forney Young b. in Baltimore, Md. April 17, 1871

Elizabeth Forney Young b. in Baltimore, Md., Jan 26, 1874

Jacob Forney Young b. in Baltimore, Md., Oct 28, 1875

Robert Forney Young b. in Baltimore, Md., May 8, 1880

William Piatt Young, first son of Temperance Butler and Jacob Forney Young, b. near Hagerstown, Md., Aug 12, 1909.

Temperance Glenn Young, first dau. of Temperance B. Young and Jacob F. Young b. Oct 5, 1912.

Jacob Forney Young, Jr., second son of Temperance Butler Young and Jacob Forney Young b. Hagerstown, Md., 326 Summit Ave., Jan 8, 1919.

William Piatt Young, Jr., first son of William Piatt Young and Margaret Ann Moore b. at Hagerstown (Washington Co. Hospital) on Feb 26, 1940.

Ann Forney Young, first dau. of Wm. Piatt Young and Ann Moore Young, b. at Washington Co. Hospital, Hagerstown, Md., Sep 13, 1944.

Jacob Forney Young, III, first son of Jacob Forney Young, Jr. and Hannah Kingston Young b. at St. Vincent's Hospital, N.Y. City, Nov 27, 1947.

DEATHS

Grace Young d. in Baltimore, Md. Jan 26, 1864, aged 11 months and 28 days (Consumption).

Mary A. Young d. Baltimore, on Apr 8, 1864 aged 34 years, 2 months and 15 days (Consumption).

Charles Young d. in Hanover, Pa. of consumption on July 9, 1871 in the 23rd year of his age.

George Young, second son of William Sholl and Mary Hilt Young d. in Hanover, Pa., Oct 16, 1895, aged 42 years, 4 months, 19 days.

William Forney Young d. in Hanover, Pa. of disease of the brain on Jan 4, 1872 aged 8 months, 18 days.

Robert Forney Young d. in Baltimore, Md., July 4, 1880 of whooping cough, aged 8 weeks and 1 day.

William Sholl Young, eldest son of George and Susan Sholl Young, d. at Sudbrook Park, Baltimore Co., Md. June 30, 1902 of paralysis; aged 76 years, 6 months and 5 days.

Lizzie Forney Young, wife of George Young, d. in Hanover, Pa. on Feb 2, 1906 aged 59 years, 3 months.

Emelia Forney Young, wife of Wm. Sholl Young, d. in Baltimore, Md., May 20, 1917, aged 75 years, 10 months, 6 days.

Emily Jane Young d. in Hanover, Pa., youngest child of George and Susan Sholl Young.

Jacob Forney Young, second son of William School Young d. at Avalon Manor, Hagerstown, Md. Feb 7, 1961, aged 85 years, 3 months, 9 days.

Temperance Butler Young, wife of Jacob Forney Young, d. at Avalon Manor, Hagerstown, Md. Aug 12, 1962, aged 79 years, 10 months, 9 days.

Louise C. Etzler d. in Hanover, Pa. on Sep 29, 1891 aged 67 yrs., 10 mos., 11 days, eldest dau. of George and Susan Sholl Young.

John S. Young, fourth and youngest son of Susan Sholl and Geo. Young, d. Hanover, Pa. of appendicitis, Oct 1900.

Reuben Young, second son of Susan Sholl and George Young, d. in Hanover, Pa. on Nov 6, 1912, aged 84 years, 11 months and 14 days.

Bentz Bible

These records were copied from the front page of a German Bible, printed in Somerset, Penna., 1813 or 1815, and sold by Bob Creager, Funkstown, Md, May 21, 1966

Cathrine Bentz, b. Jan 31, 1789

Elisabeth Bentz, b. June 30, 1795

Sally Bentz, b. Dec 11, 1799

These two baptismal records were copied from Baptismal Certificates given to the Historical Society by Mrs. Robert H. Spahr.

Martha Alice Hoover Confirmed June 9, 1867 in St. Peter's Lutheran Church (Beard's) By the Rev. M. C. Horine.

George H. Spahr Confirmed Apr 19, 1879 in St. James Church, Codorus Township, York Co., Penna. by the Rev W. H. Ketterman

(Parents of Robert H. Spahr)

Schleich Bible [Editor's note: Schleich was also spelled Schleigh in the copy to follow]

Copied from the Schleich (Bible) Heidelberg Catechism, printed in German 1800 Written by Georg Gottfreid Otterbein, Preacher at Duisburg am Rhein.

John Schleigh b. Mar 7, 1771

Mary Schleigh (formerly Stemble) b. Sep 10, 1774

And we were married Aug 4, 1793 by the Rev. M. Rahauser of Hagerstown.

Daniel H. Schleigh maried Jul 12, 1831 to Mary (or Marg.) A. Beck, daughter of L. Mayberry of Frederick at 5 o'clock a.m. by Rev. D. Schafer.

Cora m. on Tuesday Sep 18, 77 by Rev Keifaver(?)

T. E. Schleigh and E. M. Krebs m. in Chambersburg on Sunday July 25, 1833 by the Rev. Fred. Rahauser.

BIRTHS

William Schleich b. Aug 23, 1794, 6 o'clock

John Schleich b. Feb 27, 1797 at 6 o'clock A.M.

Ana Mary Schleich b. Feb 19, 1799, at 9 o'clock P.M.

Samuel Henry Schleigh b. Nov 23, 1803

Daniel Henry Schleigh b. Nov 9, 1807, P.M.

An Leutrisha Schleich b. Mar 29, 1810 A.M.

Thomas Eloia Schleich b. Mar 16, 1813, P.M.

Jacob Brown Schleich b. Aug 20, 1814

Christina Rebeka b. Oct 8, 1817

Josephen Schleigh b. Sep 28, 1829

Morgerits um halb 8 ufn gedauft Dec 26, 1817

Mary Clorinda Rebeca Schleigh b. May 12, 1832, Sunday morning 3 1/2 o'clock

Frederick Washington Schleigh b. Dec 12, 1835, 5 A.M.

Lucretia Sophia Schleigh b. Jan 14, 1836 10 minutes after 1 in the morning

Ellen Alcinda Schleigh b. Nov 22, 1837 1/2 past five in the evening in a tremendous storm.

From the Family Bible of Joseph and Mary H. Garver

Joseph Garver and Mary Holmes m. Sep 4, 1828

BIRTHS

Joseph Garver b. June 12, 1803

Mary Garver b. July 28, 1804

Their Children:

John W. Garver b. June 14, 1829

Isaac S. Garver b. May 15, 1831

Ann Rebecca Garver b. Nov 22, 1833

Joseph Garver b. Feb 16, 1836

Daniel N. or H. Garver b. Feb 17, 1838

Samuel Garver b. May 16, 1843

DEATHS

Isaac S. Garver d. in the State of "Mosouri", Nov 11, 1864

Mary Garver d. Aug 27, 1869

Joseph Garver d. Apr 25, 1870

Samuel B. Garver d. Aug 24, 1907

Joseph Garver d. Jun 25, 1908

From the Family Bible of Joseph Little, 1850

Joseph Little and Susana Groscost, his wife, m. Feb 22, 1786 by the Rev. Cobbreght.

Joseph Little b. Sep 16, 1766

Susana Little b. May 1767, d. Oct 2, 1836

John Little b. 1786 and d. Aug 19, 1805

Joseph Little b. Feb 4, 1788

Jacob Little b. Oct 29, 1789

Adam Little b. Dec 10, 1790

Susana Little b. Feb 10, 1792

Christianna Little b. Feb 5, 1794, d. Dec 17, 1825

Elizabeth Little b. Dec 10, 1796

David Little b. Apr 20, 1797.

Jesse Miller Little b. Aug 10, 1798

Mary Little b. Aug 2, 1800

William Little b. Apr 18, 1802

Elias Little b. Apr 16, 1804

Jonathan Little b. Mar 27, 1806.

Daniel Frederick Litle b. Sep 6, 1807

Joseph W. Little b. Nov 4, 1852

Joseph Little was confirmed May 23, 1819 by the Rev. James Ross Reily, pastor of Zion Reformed Church, Hagerstown, Md.

Henry C. Zeigler b. Sep 9, 1852 near Leitersburg, Md, d. Mar 17, 1891. Married Mar 29, 1881 Alice M. Little, b. Jan 13, 1856 Hagerstown, Md.

From the Family Bible of "Dan'l and E. Dunn."

(Title page missing)

MARRIAGES

Daniel Dunn and Elizabeth Schindel m. Dec 12, 1839

BIRTHS

Daniel Dunn b. Feb 25, 1808

Elizabeth Dunn b. Oct 30, 1811

Mary Catherine Dunn b. Nov 17, 1840

Elizabeth Ellen Dunn b. Mar 25, 1842

Amelia Jane Dunn b. Mar 2, 1844

Arabell Dunn b. May 6, 1846

Alice Margret Dunn b. July 22, 1848

William Hollen Dunn b. Jan 26, 1851

John P. Dunn b. Jan 8, 1853

Edwin Preston Dunn b. Jan 22, 1857

DEATHS

Mother, Elizabeth Dunn d. Apr 8, 1861, 49 yrs, 5 mos., 8 das.

John P. Dunn d. Nov 15, 1856, 3 yrs., 10 mos., 27 das.

Catherine Dunn d. June 9, 1892

Father, Daniel Dunn, Feb 25, 1808 - Apr 26, 1893

William H. Dunn d. Oct 23, 1901

Elizabeth E. Muselman d. Dec 5, 1872, 30 yrs, 8 mos., 5 das.

From an early Snyder Bible

Elizabeth Stouffer, wife of Jacob Snyder was b. Aug 17, 1794

Jacob S. Snyder b. Oct 12, 1793

John Snyder b. June 10, 1826

Samuel Snyder b. Aug 11, 1827

Jacob Snyder b. June 24, 1829

Amanuel Snyder b. Jan 22, 1831

DEATHS

Elizabeth Snyder, wife of Jacob Snyder, d. Aug 4, 1858

Jacob S. Snyder d. Aug 30, 1864

From Family Bible of Mary Snyder

(Holman's Edition of Holy Bible, published Phila. 1877)

Mary Catherine Snyder, Presented by her Mother Oct 27, 1880

MARRIAGES

Edward Funk of Washington Co. and Mary K. Snyder of Washington Co. at home of bride m. Jan 10, 1882 by Rev J. Spangler Kieffer. Witnesses: Albert J. Snyder and Mollie C. Spielman

BIRTHS

Edward Funk b. Mar 18, 1853

Mary K. Snyder b. Oct 27, 1860

Mary S. Funk b. October 18, 1882

Edward Richard Funk b. Nov 29, 1891

DEATHS

Edward Funk d. May 25, 1897

From the Bible of Charles J. Grove

(Wilmore's New Analytical Bible, published New York, 1893)

Grand Parents

John Peltz, b. Feb 21, 1799, d. Sep 21, 1876

Nancy Peltz, b. July 24, 1806, Hagerstown, d. Oct 20, 1888

Both died in Hagerstown, Md.

Parents

James M. Grove, b. Feb 4, 1828, d. Sep 19, 1884

Catherine Grove, b. Oct 24, 1825; d. Oct 24, 1903

Both died in Hagerstown, Md. Married in Hagerstown, Feb 19, 1852 by Rev. F. R. Auspach.

Children

Annie P. Grove, b. in Martinsburg June 20, 1853, m. Thomas A. Hartley, May 1872; d. Aug 25, 1911

John A. Grove, b. Aug 20, 1855 in Marsh, Pa.; d. June 25, 1875

Florence E. Grove, b. Hagerstown, Feb 25, 1857; d. Apr 7, 1923

James M. Grove, b. Leitersburg, Feb 2, 1859; d. Apr 6, 1928

Charles J. Grove, b. Hagerstown, June 3, 1861; d. Apr 10, 1925, m. Annie

E. Snyder, Dec 15, 1897

Genarion B. Grove, b. Funkstown, Nov 17, 1862; d. June 7, 1911

Fannie M. Grove, b. Funkstown, July 12, 1870; d. Oct 16, 1896, m. Daniel Stover, Oct 24, 1895

Jacob H. Snyder b. June 24, 1829; d. May 24, 1888, Shiloh

Anna Mary Spessard, b. Mar 31, 1834; d. Mar 2, 1916, Hagerstown, m. Nov 16, 1852

Children

John Snyder b. May 21, 1853; d. June 16, 1854

Oliver Snyder b. Oct 1, 1854; d. Jan 10, 1900

Luther S. Snyder b. Jul 2, 1856; d. Dec 29, 1939

Samuel C. Snyder b. June 9, 1858

Mary K. Snyder b. Oct 27, 1860 at Shiloh; d. May 13, 1951, m. Jan 1882 Edward Funk

Jacob E. Snyder b. Mar 25, 1862; d. Aug 1, 1862

Albert H. Snyder b. June 19, 1863; d. Jan 11, 1905

Harvey E. Snyder b. Dec 10, 1865; d. Aug 18, 1866

Icia M. Snyder b. Aug 27, 1867; d. July 21, 1963, m. Feb 3, 1892 H. L. Miner of Waynesboro, Pa.

Anna E. Snyder b. Sep 27, 1869; d. Jan 21, 1957, m. Dec 15, 1897 Charles J. Grove

William H. Snyder b. Feb 18, 1871; d. Sep 19, 1950

Charles G. Snyder b. July 17, 1873; d. March 20, 1897

Virgia O. Snyder b. June 15, 1875; d. June 21, 1876

Gertia M. Snyder b. June 15, 1875; d. Aug 3, 1876

Clifford S. Snyder b. July 12, 1877

Bessie E. Snyder b. July 12, 1877

Grandparents

James M. Grove b. Feb 4, 1828; d. Sep 19, 1884, Hagerstown

Catherine Grove b. Oct 24, 1825; d. Oct 24, 1903

Jacob H. Snyder b. June 24, 1829; d. May 24, 1888, Shiloh

Anna Mary Snyder b. Mar 31, 1834; d. Mar 8, 1916, Hagerstown

Parents

Charles J. Grove b. June 3, 1861 Hagerstown, d. Apr 10, 1825

Annie E. Grove b. Sep 27, 1869 Fiddlersburg, d. Jan 21, 1957

Hagerstown, m. Dec 15, 1897, Baltimore, Md. by Rev. Herbert Richardson

Children

Charles P. Grove b. Sep 14, 1902 Hagerstown

From Family Bible of John H. Funk

(Published Philadelphia by Charles H. Yost, Bible Publisher, 1217 Market Street)

Certificate of Church Membershp - Ann Virginia Winters, May 25, 1862 by J. W. Santee, Pastor of German Reformed Congregation, Cavetown, Md.

Confirmation Record - Johannus Funk, June 10, 1821, Signed by James R. Reily, V.D.M. (Grandfather of John H. Funk, 1844-1938)

Certificate of Church Membership - Miss Catherine Funk, May 7, 1859 signed by ___ Giesy, Pastor of German Reformed Congregation, Hagerstown, Md.

BIRTHS

John Henry Funk b. Mar 26, 1844

Ann Virginia Funk b. Mar 20, 1848

Elvin Winters Funk b. May 12, 1875

Flavia Fanetta Funk b. Nov 3, 1876

John Kieffer Funk b. Apr 7, 1879

Margie May Funk b. Dec 14, 1882

Henry Seth Funk b. June 14, 1888

MARRIAGES

John H. Funk m. Ann V. Winters, Feb 5, 1874 by J. W. Santee, Pastor Reformed Church, Cavetown

Margie May Funk and Harry K. Young, June 1, 1904

John Kieffer Funk and Maud Wolf, Aug 4, 1906

Elvin Winters Funk and Bessie Lee Hartle, Jan 15, 1908

Henry Seth Funk and Mary Virginia Harshman, Mar 31, 1920

DEATHS

Ann Virginia Funk, July 28, 1912, aged 64 years

John H. Funk, Oct 10, 1938, aged 94 years

Margie M. Funk Young, Nov 4, 1938, aged 55 years

Elvin Winters Funk, May 25, 1944, aged 69 years

Bessie L. Hurtle Funk, Oct 8, 1944, aged 70 years

Henry Seth Funk, Mar 7, 1957, aged 69 years

John Kieffer Funk, Nov 20, 1966, aged 87 years, 7 months, 13 days

Flavia F. Funk, June 1, 1955

From Family Bible of Louisa Jane Funk Wolf

BIRTHS

Henry C. Wolf b. Jan 25, 1855

Louisa J. Wolf b. June 5, 1853

Infant b. Nov 6, 1882

Maud Wolf b. July 21, 1884

Frank Wolf b. July 21, 1886

John Kieffer Funk b. Apr 7, 1879

Anna Louise Funk b. June 17, 1907

Henry Wolf Funk b. June 16, 1914

Maud Elizabeth Funk b. Oct 20, 1920

DEATHS

Infant d. Nov 6, 1882

Lelia G. Zigler d. Nov 24, 1883 aged 6 yrs, 3 mos., 19 das.

Frank Wolf d. Jan 30, 1890, 3 yrs, 6 mos., 9 das.

Henry C. Wolf d. Aug 11, 1927 aged 72 yrs., 6 mos., 16 das.

Louisa J. Wolf d. Jan 14, 1937 aged 83 yrs., 5 mos., 9 das.

Joseph S. Wolf d. Oct 22, 1934; b. Dec 31, 1857

J. Kieffer Funk d. Nov 20, 1966 aged 87 yrs., 7 mos., 13 das.

MARRIAGES
Henry C. Wolf m. Louisa Funk Feb 4, 1879

Maud Wolf m. J. Kieffer Frank Aug 4, 1906

From the Family Bible of Samuel Isaac Funk

BIRTHS

Samuel I. Funk b. Aug 28, 1818; d. June 8, 1900

Mary Louise (Wagoner) Funk b. Feb 26, 1832; d. Apr 9, 1919

Ellen O. Funk b. Mar 28, 1849; d. Feb 22, 1903

Elizabeth Ann Funk b. May 24, 1850; d. Mar 29, 1896, m. Shaneberger

Catherine Virginia Funk b. Nov 20, 1851; d. 1932. (m. Wm. E. Funk, dau. Cora)

Louise Jane Funk b. June 5, 1853; d. Jan 14, 1939, m. Wolf

Martin Alvey Funk b. Jan 13, 1855; d. Sep 13, 1856

William Otho Funk b. Aug 14, 1857 buried at Rose Hill

Ellsworth Hooker Funk b. Aug 6, 1861; d. Mar 3, 1864

Isouria Bell Funk (Kaylor) b. Feb 1, 1863; d. 1930

Clara Editha Funk b. Oct 5, 1868; d. Apr 10, 1951. (m. Chas. A. Weagly, son Roy)

Andrew Funk (brother of Samuel) d. Mar 22, 1902 aged 90 yrs., 6 mos, 21 days, wife Katie Doub Funk d. Feb 19, 1892 aged 22 yrs., 9 mos., 28 days, daughter Sarilla K. Funk b. Jan 3, 1844; d. Mar 29, 1915

daughter Ella Funk b. Rose Hill m. George Bovey (bros. Luther, Ed; s. Mrs. John Bentz, Mrs. Lily Rohrer); dau. Grace Bovey m. John Smith, dau. Ella Smith; Edna Bovey m. Brayden Ridenour

MARRIAGES

Samuel I. Funk m. Mary L. Wagoner, Feb 10, 1848

Ellen O. Funk m. Mahlon Newcomer, Dec 17, 1868

Elizabeth Ann Funk m. Lewis Shaneberger Feb 27, 1872

Catherine Virginia Funk m. Wm. E. Funk Nov 18, 1873

Louisa Jane Funk m. Henry C. Wolf Feb 4, 1879

William O. Funk m. Alice Rohrer Dec 16, 1879

Isouria B. Funk m. (blank) Kaylor Mar 26, 1883

Clara Edith Funk m. Charles A. Weagly Feb 12, 1885

Line of Catherine Thomas and Joseph M. Wolf -

Sisters of Catherine Thomas: Rose Ann Thomas m. Stover or Stouffer, Elizabeth Thomas m. Hurley, Susan Thomas m. Waltz, Cynthia Thomas m. Friese, brothers; Jacob Thomas, Jack Thomas, Yoney(?) Thomas, John Thomas went West

Line of John Wolf

1. Joseph Wolf b. Dec 18, 1783; d. Aug 18, 1869 wife Elenorah Zuck b. Mar 3, 1770; d. Dec 9, 1859

2. Daniel Wolf

3. John Wolf

4. Elizabeth Wolf Fasnaught

5. Susan Wolf Shector

6. Hannah Wolf

   II-1. Elizabeth Wolf, b. Sep 8, 1809 - Aug 1, 1832; m. Peter Middlekauff (went to Illinois)

   III-1. Simon P. Middlekauff b. July 25, 1832 wife Jeanna

   IV-1. Alice, 2. Charles d. Nov 5, 1864, 3. Daniel, 4. Florence d. May 7, 1869, 5. Joseph

   II-2. Joseph Maxwell Wolf b. June 9, 1816; d. May 3, 1873; w. Catherine Thomas b. Oct 13, 1815; d. Dec 25, 1876

   III-1. Hiram J. Wolf Dec 29, 1837; d. Oct 1897

   IV-1. Fred J. Wolf, 1886; 2. Carry Wolf Stump, 1870-1924; 3. Harry T. Wolf 1875-1950; 4. Walter C. Wolf 1878-1916; 5. Morris H. Wolf 1882-1958 m. Elna Wright of Chicago

   V-1. Harriet b. 1920

   6. Nellie K. Wolf 1884; 7. Grace S. Wolf Lightfoot 1884

   III-2. Susan E. Wolf July 30, 1840-May 9, 1850

III-3. Elizabeth C. Wolf Mar 9, 1845 - Jan 19, 1874; m. 1867 Samuel Martin

IV-1. William Martin 1868; 2. Joseph Martin 1871; 3. Lizzie Martin 1875; 4. Infant 1871

III-4. Jacob I. Wolf b. Nov 13, 1848; d. Dec 21, 194-; m.

IV-1. Leona Wolf m. Chas. Rinehart; 2. Abner S. Wolf; 3. William Wolf; 4. Joseph Wolf; 5. Henry Wolf

III-5. Henry C. Wolf b. Jan 25, 1855; d. Aug 11, 1927

IV-1. Maud Wolf July 21, 1884 m. J. Keiffer Funk

IV-2. Frank Wolf July 21, 1886 - Jan 30, 1890

IV-3. Infant

III-6. Joseph S. Wolf Dec 31, 1857 - Oct 22, 1934

Stones in Beaver Creek Cemetery

John Wolf d. Mar 13, 1819 aged 58-6-22

Daniel Wolf, son of John and Catherine Wolf d. Feb 18, 1853 aged 28 yrs, 10 mos. 12 days

Benjamin Franklin, son of John S. and Martha or Madeline Wolf d. Oct 21, 1863, aged 21 yrs. 21 days

Family of Charles Rinehart b. Aug 29, 1874 and Leona Wolf Rinehart b. Oct 13, 1874

Children:

1. Henry Luther Rinehart 1898-1952, m. Ethel Yessler
2. Mildred Loraine Rinehart 1900 -, m. J. E. Ground (Ft. Lauderdale, Fla.
3. Bruce Theron Rinehart 1902 -, m. Katherine Haishman; child: 1) Theron, 2) Deloris, 3) Sigie
4. Donald Joseph Rinehart 1905 -, m. Delva Conley
5. Charles Wolf Rinehart 1908
6. Jacob Lewis Rinehart 1911 -, m. Argie Prosper (N. Colonial Dr.); son William Newton Rinehart 1938 -
7. Joseph Alan Rinehart 1915

Newcomer Records

Records in possession of Mrs. Kieffer Funk

BIRTHS

John Newcomer b. Dec 18, 1797

Catherine Newcomer b. Dec 18, 1802

Elizabeth Ann Newcomer b. Dec 3, 1824

Benjamin Franklin Newcomer b. Apr 28, 1827

John Henry Newcomer b. July 7, 1829

Alexander Newcomer b. Aug 3, 1831

A son b. June 26, 1834 and d. June 29, 1834

William Newcomer b. Aug 13, 1835

Ellen Newcomer b. July 14, 1838

Mary Newcomer b. Sep 29, 1840

MARRIAGES

John Newcomer m. Catharine Newcomer Dec 12, 1822

Lewis Ripple m. Elizabeth A. Newcomer Feb 14, 1850

Benj. F. Newcomer m. Amelia Louise Ehlen, in Baltimore, Nov 14, 1848

John Henry Newcomer m. O. Ella Williams, Apr 1, 1858

William Newcomer m. Eliza H. Witmer May, 1859

Mary Newcomer m. Charles McCauley, Jan 8, 1861

DEATHS

Elizabeth A. Ripple d. Dec 11, 1856 aged 32 years, 8 days

John Newcomer d. Apr 21, 1861 aged 63 yrs, 4 mos., 3 days

John Henry Newcomer d. Jan 26, 1877 aged 47 yrs, 6 mos., 19 days

Mary McCauley d. June 21, 1896 aged 55, yrs., 8 mos, 21 days

Benjamin Franklin Newcomer d. Mar 30, 1901 aged 73 yrs., 11 mos., 2 days

Catharine Newcomer died Feb 3, 1883 aged 80 yrs, 1 mo, 15 days

Witmer Records

From records in possession of Mrs. J. Kieffer Funk

BIRTHS

Benjamin Witmer b. Sep 14, 1808

Catherine Witmer b. Aug 27, 1811

Eleanora Witmer b. Aug 16, 1835

Eliza Witmer b. Dec 16, 1836

Mary Louise Wagoner b. Feb 26, 1832 m. Samuel Isaac Funk (grandmother of Mrs. J. K. Junk)

John Witmer, Sr. b. May 1, 1774

Barbara Witmer b. Apr 15, 1774

MARRIAGES

Benjamin Witmer m. Catharine Hammond Dec 16, 1832

Samuel Funk m. Mary L. Wagoner, Feb 16, 1848

William Newcomer m. Eliza Witmer Apr 26, 1859

John Witmer m. Barbara Newcomer Jan 1, 1795

DEATHS

Elenora Witmer d. aged 4, Dec 16, 1835

Barbara Witmer d. May 1, 1837 aged 64

Ann Witmer d. Feb 1, 1845 aged 57

Henry Witmer d. Feb 16, 1840 aged 60

John Witmer d. Aug 11, 1858 aged 84 yrs, 3 mos. 10 days

Ann Witmer d. Nov 20, 1859 aged 49 yrs., 7 mos.

David Witmer d. Apr 8, 1862 aged 56 yrs.

Mary Witmer d. May, 1852 aged 45 years

Mary Witmer, wife of John Witmer, Sr. d. Sep 12, 1890

Benjamin Witmer d. Mar 18, 1879 aged 70 years, 6 mos, 5 days

Catherine Witmer d. July 26, 1894 aged 82 yrs, 11 mos., 29 days

Benjamin Witmer, son of Henry, d. July 17, 1814 aged 18 years

Musser Witmer d. --- 18, 1816, aged 21 years

Elizabeth Ross, wife of George W. Ross d. Dec 2, 1817 aged 28 years

Mary Witmer d. Nov 22, 1820

Henry Witmer, father of the above children, d. Dec 2, 1821 aged 71 years. His wife d. June 19, 1823

Records from Beaver Creek Cemetery, Church of the Brethren

Mahlon Newcomer Sep 24, 1845 - Sep 25, 1922, wife Ellen O. Funk Newcomer, Mar 28, 1849 - Feb 22, 1903; son Howard Newcomer, only child

son Dorsey

dau. Thelma Newcomer Smith

Charles A. Weagley, Nov 19, 1863 - Apr 23, 1948
Clara Editha Funk Weagley, Oct 5, 1868 - Apr 10, 1951
Roy C. F. Weagley, Sep 4, 1885
Maude A. C. Eccard Weagly, Aug 8, 1886 - Aug 17, 1957
Roger Funk Weagly, May 27, 1911 - Aug 15, 1929; son of Roy and Maude Weagly.

Isouria Bell Funk Kaylor, Feb 1, 1863 - 1930; dau. Mary R. Kaylor 1889 - 1911
(Isouria Kaylor mother of Harry Kaylor and sister of Clara Weagly and Louisa Jane Funk)
John W. Kaylor 1850 - 1912

William E. Funk 1846 - 1922; w. Catherine Virginia Funk, Nov 20, 1851 - 1932; infant dau. 1881 - 1881
dau. Cora M. Funk Feb 1883

Samuel J. Funk, Aug 28, 1818 - June 8, 1900; wife Mary L. Wagoner Funk, m. Feb 10, 1848; Feb 26, 1832 - Apr 9, 1919

dau. Elizabeth Ann Funk Shaneberger - no issue; May 24, 1850 - Mar 29, 1896; (husband Lewis R. Shaneberger - not buried at Beaver Creek - had second wife)
son Martin Alvey Funk, Jan 13, 1855, d. in infancy
son William Otho Funk, Aug 14, 1857 buried Rose Hill
son Ellsworth Hooker Funk, Aug 6, 1860, d. in infancy

dau. Louisa Jane Funk Wolf
dau. Isouria Bell Funk Kaylor
dau. Catherine Virginia Funk Funk
dau. Clara Editha Funk Weagley

Andrew Funk, (brother of Samuel), d. Mar 22, 1902 aged 90 years, 6 months, 21 days; wife Katie Doub Funk d. Feb 19, 1892 aged 22 years, 9 months, 28 days
d.[daughter] Savilla K. Funk Jan 3, 1844 - Mar 29, 1915
John Funk Sep 5, 1789 - Oct 27, 1877
Catherine, wife of John Funk, Dec 17, 1799 - Jan 28, 1862 (nee Newcomer)
d.[daughter] Ann Maria Funk Oct 28, 1827 - Aug 9, 1898

Henry C. Wolf Jan 25, 1855 - Aug 11, 1927
Louisa Jane Funk Wolf June 5, 1853 - Jan 14, 1937; son Frank Wolf, d. Jan 30, 1890 aged 3 years, 6 months, 2 days
adopted dau. Lelia G. Zigler, d. Nov 24, 1883 aged 6 years
Infant son d. Nov 6, 1883

Joseph S. Wolfe (brother of Henry C.), Dec 31, 1857 - Oct 22, 1934
Catherine Thomas Wolf wife of Joseph M. Wolf d. Dec 25, 1876 aged 61 years, 2 months, 12 days
Joseph Maxwell Wolf, June 9, 1816 - May 3, 1873

Elizabeth C. Wolf Martin (only sister of Henry C. Wolf) wife of Samuel Martin (he remarried & went to California)
Elizabeth Martin d. Jan 19, 1874 aged 28 years, 10 months, 10 days
Infant son, Joseph A. d. Dec 20, 1871 aged 2 years, 13 days
Infant d. Nov 20, 1871 aged 9 days

Old Stones in Beaver Creek near Church of the Brethren

Jacob L. Funk Sep 7, 1863 or 1803, aged 43 years, 4 months, 28 days (very old stone)
Caroline --- of Jacob Funk
John Wolf d. Mar 13, 1819?, aged 58 years, 6 months, 22 days
Daniel, son of John and Catherine Wolfe, d. Feb 18, 1853 aged 28 years, 10 months, 12 days
Benjamin Franklin, son of John S. and Martha (or Madeline) Wolf, d. Oct 21, 1863 aged 21 years, 27 days

Records from the Family Bible of S. Milford Schindel by permission of Anna Catherine Roulette Wagaman

MARRIAGES

S. Milford Schindel m. Annie E. Biendle Feb 17, 1876

George Schindel m. Camilla Winders Jan 16, 1847

Parents of: Samuel Milford Schindel b. Nov 1, 1847; Oscar M. Schindel b. Oct 14, 1849; Norman E. Schindel b. Feb 10, 1851; Ida Camilla Schindel, died.

William U. Roulette and Bertha Elizabeth Schindel, Feb 19, 1901.

Gail Madison Hamill and Camilla F. Schindel m. Aug 12, 1908 and went to S. Dakota.

BIRTHS

George Schindel b. Jan 16, 1818, son of Samuel Schindel and Julia Hade Schindel

Samuel Schindel, son of Ludwig Schindel of Hanover, York Co., Pa.

Julia Hade dau. of Johan Hade, Franklin Co, Pa,

Camilla Winders, dau. of Samuel Winders, Somerset Co., Penna. and Susan Newcomer, Beaver Creek, Md., wife of George Schindel (Mother of S. Milford Schindel)

Samuel Milford Schindel b. Nov 1, 1847

Annie Elizabeth Brendle b. Jan 16, 1852, wife of S. Milford Schindel

Son, Guy Roman Schindel b. Jan 27, 1877

Dau. Bertha Elizabeth Schindel b. Feb 7, 1880

Dau. Camilla Frances Schindel b. Dec 7, 1883 (in the morning)

Dau. Charlotte Esther Schindel b. Feb 9, 1889 (in the morning)

DEATHS

Guy Roman Schindel, d. Aug 5, 1877 aged 6 mos. 9 days

Charlotte Esther Schindel d. May 9, (1903), aged 14 years, 3 mos. of malignant sore throat, sick for 4 days.

Camilla Schindel Hamill d. July 9, 1910 aged 26 years, 7 mos. 20 days, cancer, at home, 919 Maryland Avenue, Hagerstown, Md. wife of Gail M. Hamill of Hamill Tripp Co., S. Dakota.

Bertha Elizabeth Schindel Roulette, d. Sep 6, 1939 of a heart attack.

From the Holy Bible of Sarah Reilly

Bible owned by Sarah Reilly

In possession of Mrs. John Dunn, Hagerstown, Md.

BIRTHS

Dr. J. S. Maurer, Assistant Surgeon, U. S. Army, b. Nov 21, 1837, Hagerstown, Md.

Catherine Riley b. Aug 31, 1839

William H. Dunn b. Jan 29, 1851

Laura V. Dunn b. Sep 7, 1854

Sons: Clyde Riley Dunn b. Sunday, Nov 7, 1875, Washington Co., Md.

John Daniel Dunn b. July 5, 1885, Hagerstown, Md.

MARRIAGES

Dr. J. S. Maurer to Catherine Riley Oct 21, 1863

D. D. Riley m. Josie E. Dick Aug 2, 1877

Alfonsus Faller m. Mary Ellen Riley, Nov 3, 1869

R. W. Ensminger m. Jennie Belle Riley, June 1, 1881

F. W. Stover m. Lottie Alice Riley Oct 2, 1878

Laura V. Riley m. W. H. Dunn Mar 27, 1875

From a loose page found in Bible - J. S. Jamure, Asst. Surg, U. S. Army and Kate Riley m. Oct 21, 1863 at Easton, Penna by Wm. L. Grant, Minister of the Gospel

BIRTHS

John Riley b. Nov 13, 1812

Sarah Stone b. Nov 29, 1819

Michael Stone b. Mar 3, 1797

Catherine Stone b. July 13, 1799

Margaret Ann Stone b. May 5, 1809

Francis Stone b. Mar 20, 1841

Catherine Riley b. Aug 31, 1839

Margaret Ann Riley b. Feb 10, 1841

Dennis De Witt Riley b. May 17, 1844

John Clayton Riley b. Sep 5 [Ed. note: no year given.]

Mary Ellen Riley b. Sep 14, 1847

William Riley b. Sep 3, 1849

BIRTHS

Lottie Alice Riley b. Aug 1, 1851

Laura Virginia Riley b. Sep 7, 1853

Jennie Belle Riley b. Feb 10, 1859

George W. Riley b. Feb 10, 1862

DEATHS

John Riley d. Jan 8, 1887

Mrs. Sarah Riley d. Apr 18, 1888

William Riley

Mollie Riley

Dennis D. Riley

Kate Maurer d. Nov 19, 1919

Laura V. Dunn d. Jan 31, 1929

Clyde Riley Dunn d. Dec 29, 1883

The following Bible records are copied from the Bible owned by Lilian Schindel Taylor - a loan to Elizabeth S. Roulette

Copied by Mrs. Frank S. Schwartz by permission of Anna Catharine Roulette Wagaman (Mrs. James Wagaman), August 14, 1972

George Shindel b. Jan 14, 1818

Jonathan Shindel b. Sep 20, 1819

Lewis Shindel b. Jan 6, 1821

Ann Maria Shindel b. Feb 3, 1822

Elizabeth Shindel b. June 3, 1823

Rebecca Cathrine Shindel b. Mar 21, 1825

Samuel Shindel b. July 24, 1826

Andrew Shindel b. June 17, 1828

Ana Amelia Shindel b. Jan 24, 1830

Adline Eve Shindel b. Oct 21, 1831

Louisa Sophiah Shindel b. May 14, 1833

Jacob Henry Shindel b. Mar 24, 1836

Samuel Schindel b. Dec 23, 1791

Julia Anna Schnindel b. July 6, 1797

DEATHS

Jonathan Shindel d. Feb 10, 1884, aged 64 yrs. 4 mos. 20 days

Elizabeth Brewer (Shindel) d. Feb 19, 1884, aged 60 yrs. 8 mos. 16 days

Rebecca Catharine Shindel d. Sep 2, 1826, aged 1 yr. 5 mos. 12 days

Samuel E. Shindel d. Apr 24, 1900

Adline Eve Shindel d. Oct 12, 1836, aged 4 yrs 11 mos. 21 days

Louisa Sophiah Schindel d. Feb 22, 1866, aged 32 yrs. 9 mos. 5 days

Samuel Schindel d. Aug 14, 1863 at 9 p.m., aged 72 yrs 7 mos. 14 days

Julia Anna Schindel d. Oct 19, 1858, aged 61 yrs. 3 mos. 17 days

Andrew Jackson Schindel d. Jan 15, 1915

[These records were translated from a page of the Bible that was written in German. A copy of the German writing and the translation of it are found pasted in the notebook on pp. 126-127. [at the Washington Co. Historical Society] Also, there is a copy of the front page of the Bible which was in German and published in Lancaster, Pa. in 1819]

Samuel Schindel m. Julien Heth Feb 1, 1817

Children: George Schindel b. Jan 14, 1818

Jonathan Schindel b. Sep 20, 1819

Ludwig Schindel b. Jan 6, 1821

Anmaria Schindel b. Feb 3, 1822

Elizabeth Schindel b. June 3, 1823

Rebecka Schindel b. Mar 21, 1825

Daniel Schindel b. July 24, 1826

Andreas Schindel b. June 17, 1828

William Schindel b. Jan 24, 1830

Etleina Efa Schindel b. Oct 21, 1831

Louisa Sofia Schindel b. May 14, 1833

Jacob Henry Schindel b. Mar 24, 1836

Katrina Merkred b. June 11 (no year given)

Kadiele Scheni b. Feb 2, (no year given)

Zug - Wolf Line

Daniel Wolf and Ann Maria Rowland m. Oct 15, 1850

William R. Wolf and Susan Jane Young m. Dec 23, 1879

Samuel H. Neikirk m. Nancy Catherine Wolf Dec 13, 1881

John Shively Wolf m. Mary Ellen Yountz m. Jan 14, 1885

Charles Thomas Mumma m. Susan Isabell Wolf Jan 20, 1890

Joseph Daniel Wolf m. Edna C. Long Dec 5, 1894

Ellen M. Wolf m. Aaron M. Mullindore Dec 14, 1886

DEATHS

Samuel Henry Neikirk d. Aug 22, 1926 aged 71 yrs. 4 days

Charles Thomas Mumma d. Nov 16, 1926, aged 60 yrs. 8 mos. 6 days

Isabell Levinia Wolf d. June 3, 1909

Susan Wolf d. Oct 10, 1839 aged 41 yrs. 6 mos. 1 day

David Wolf d. Apr 17, 1845 aged 52 yrs. 8 mos. 15 days

Sarah Jane Wolf d. July 9, 1864 aged 1 yr. 8 mos. 15 das.

Ellen M. Mullindore d. Feb 4, 1888 aged 23 yrs. 1 mo. 14 days

BIRTHS

David Wolf b. Aug 6, 1793
Susan Wolf b. Mar 15, 1798
Daniel Wolf b. Aug 11 1825 or 1827
Ann Maria Rowland b. Dec 11, 1828
Emma Cora Wolf b. Oct 10, 1851
William Rowland Wolf b. Sep 11, 1853
Nancy Catharine Wolf b. Dec 27, 1856
Mary Wolf b. Nov 29, 1858
John Shively Wolf b. Jan 2, 1861
Sarah Jane Wolf b. Oct 24, 1862
Ellen M. Wolf b. Dec 20, 1864
Susan Isabel Wolf b. Aug 20, 1866
Bettie Laura Wolf b. June 8, 1868
Joseph Daniel Wolf b. July 11, 1870
Fanny May Wolf b. Nov 27, 1873
Wilbur Wolf Mumma b. Feb 11, 1900

DEATHS

Daniel Wolf d. Aug 16, 1899, aged 74 yrs. 5 days
Ann Mary Wolf d. Oct 21, 1912 aged 88 years, 10 months, 2 days
Fanny May Wolf d. May 20, 1903 aged 29 years, 5 months, 23 days
Wilbur Wolf Mumma d. Aug 15, 1914 aged 14 years, 6 months, 4 days
Nannie C. Neikirk d. May 7, 1926 aged 70 years, 4 months, 17 days
Susan Isabell Mumma d. Jul 11, 1926 at 59 years, 10 months, 11 days
Emma Cora Wolf d. July 17, 1929 aged 77 years, 8 months, 7 days
William Rowland Wolf d. Mar 4, 1932 aged 78 years, 5 months, 22 days
Mary Wolf d. June 13, 1933 aged 74 years, 6 months, 14 days
Bettie Laura Wolf d. Oct 4, 1936 aged 68 years, 4 months, 26 days
Joe Wolf d. Mar 31, 1938, Thurs.
Edna Catherine Wolf d. Thurs A.M. Sep 21, 1939, Hospital, age 66 years.

Heimel Family - From notes kept by Miss Electa Ziegler

Justus Heimel b. Sep 7, 1832 and Katherine Wagner Heimel b. Jul 29, 1838 (Waggoner) m. Aug 30, 1863 by the Rev. Joshua Evans, pastor of St. John's Lutheran Church. Witness: Frank Hahn, et al. Parents of 9 children. Justus Heimel b. Herrnbreitungen, Hessen-Kessel, Germany

Mrs. Katherine Heimel's mother was Christina Lehr of Michelstadt, Hessen Darmstadt, Germany.

J. Heimel came to America 1858, d. in Hagerstown 1912.

Note "1834 the 2nd October 10 o'clock at night there is for us born into the world 2 boys, the first called Gottlob, the second Gottlieb Schmed."

Vance Family Bible

MARRIAGES

William Vance m. Elizabeth Kuhn Feb 14, 1843

Gertrude Elizabeth Schnebly m. William Grubb Vance Nov 27, 1901, Fairview, Md.

Catharine Schnebly Vance m. Ray Victor Roney Jan 27, 1923 at home 239 S. Potomac St., Hagerstown, Md.

Betty Jeannette Houser m. William Vance Roney Aug 6, 1949 Zion Lutheran Church, Williamsport, Md.

Jo Anne Roney m. Arthur Morgan Lusby, III June 3, 1972 St. John's Lutheran Church, Hagerstown, Md.

BIRTHS

William Vance b. Dec 19, 1819

Mrs. Elizabeth Vance b. Apr 3, 1822

Catherine Schnebly Vance b. Jan 27, 1904

William Vance Roney b. Apr 4, 1925

John Richard Roney b. Nov 18, 1927

Ray Victor Roney b. Jan 10, 1899

Martha Jane Vance b. Nov 16, 1843

Ann Mary Vance b. Sep 13, 1846

Andrew Snively Vance b. Oct 11, 1847

Samuel Peter Vance b. Oct 6, 1851

William Grubb Vance b. May 28, 1858

Ida Catharine Vance b. Jan 9, 1863

DEATHS

Ray Victor Roney d. May 28, 1942

John Henry Roney d. Feb 18, 1952 aged 86 years

Martha Jane Vance d. Aug 16, 1844

Ida Catharine Vance d. Sep 10, 1865

Our Father, William Vance d. June 30, 1886 aged 66 yrs. 6 mos and 11 days

Samuel Peter Vance d. Dec 17, 1921

W. G(rubb) Vance d. May 1, 1929

Gertrude Elizabeth Vance d. Nov 12, 1961 aged 92 years

Schnebly Family

MARRIAGES

Samuel R. Schnebly to Florence V. Craig, Dec 13, 1900

Gertrude E. Schnebly to William G. Vance, Nov 27, 1902

On a loose sheet of paper found in this Bible -

Lewis Resley Schnebly b. June 28, 1840

Mary Catherine Schnebly b. Feb 17, 1838 nee Middlekauff, m. Feb 28, 1867 by Rev. S. N. Calender, Reformed Minister

BIRTHS

Norman Goodrich Schnebly b. Jan 27, 1868

Gertrude Elizabeth Schnebly b. Oct 11, 1869

John Bernard Schnebly b. Apr 10, 1872

Samuel Resley Schnebly b. July 23, 1874

Clarence Middlekauff Schnebly b. July 10, 1877

Lewis Allen Schnebly b. Dec 12, 1880

Mary Louise Schnebly, dau. of Samuel and Florence Craig Schnebly b. Dec 24, 1901

DEATHS

Norman Goodrich Schnebly d. Aug 2, 1868

John Bernard Schnebly d. Nov 15, 1873

Florence Craig Schnebly, wife of Samuel Schnebly d. Dec 31, 1903

Mary Catherine Schnebly b. Feb 17, 1838, d. Nov 13, 1912

From notes of Catherine Vance Roney

John m. Lydia (Resley) Schnebly Feb 27, 1867

From Stone in St. Paul's Cemetery near Clear Spring, Md:

John Schnebly 1798 - 1876

Lydia Resley Schnebly Feb 16, 1802 - 1894

Lewis Resley Schnebly m. Mary Catherine Middlekauff dau. of ---- Barr Middlekauff, her mother of Charles Town, W.Va.

From the Family Bible of Joseph and Mary H. Garver

Joseph Garver m. Mary Holmes Sep 4, 1828

Joseph Garver b. June 12, 1803

Mary Garver b. July 28, 1804

Their Children:
John W. Garver b. June 14, 1829
Isaac S. Garver b. May 15, 1831
Anne Rebecca Garver b. Nov 22, 1833
Joseph Garver b. Feb 16, 1836
Daniel N or H. Garver b. Feb 17, 1838
Samuel Garver b. May 16, 1843

DEATHS

Isaac S. Garver d. "in the State of Mosouri, Nov 11, 1864"

Mary Garver d. Aug 27, 1869

Joseph Garver d. Apr 25, 1870

Samuel B. Garver d. Aug 24, 1907

Joseph Garver d. June 25, 1908

[The following was written in German, a copy of which is pasted in the notebook. It does not say who translated the names into English.]

Melise Bowman b. Feb 2, 1808

Emmanuel Bowman b. Aug 8, 1809

Reachel (?) Bowman b. Oct 11, 1811

Haesecia Bowman b. Oct 30, 1813

Archey Bowman b. Nov 15, 1815

Johnathun Bowman b. Dec 22, 1817

William Bowman b. Sep 20, 1819

Samuel Bowman b. May 10, 1822 or 1823

David R. Bowman b. Sep 14, 1824

Aron Bowman b. June 5, 1824

Jacob Bowman b. Sep 23, 182-

Simon Bowman b. ? 3, 1830

Elijah Bowman b. Jan 17, 18--

Andrew Bowman d. June 15, 1854

Crunkleton Family Bible

James S. Crunkleton b. Sep 5, 1836

Rebecca B. Lippy b. Sep 27, 1840

Daisy Crunkleton Shea b. May 21, 1906, Franklin Co.

Arthur Bernard Shea b. Apr 13, 1907 at Springfield, Mass.

Sally Shea Walker b. Aug 23, 1934 at Springfield, Mass.; m. Hubert Charles Walker Jan 21, 1956 by Rev. John Delany of Manchester, Connecticut

George W. Crunkleton b. Aug 6, 1862

1st wife, Mollie E. Binkley b. June 9, 1863

Dorothy Crunkleton b. Nov 11, 1916; m. Kenneth Carl Statler May 1, 1937 at Lemasters, Pa. by Rev. Edward Bieber

Herbert Walker b. Jan 17, ?

Kenneth Carl Statler b. Oct 16, 1915

MARRIAGES

James S. Crunkleton m. Rebecca B. Lippy Sep 8, 1859

George W. Crunkleton m. Mollie E. Binkley (1st wife) Feb 1, 1882

George W. Crunkleton m. Maude McLanahan (2nd wife) Sep 1, 1903 by Rev. J. B. Guiney. Certificate No. 337, Vol. 13, Chambersburg Court House.

Daisy Agnes Crunkleton m. Arthur Bernard Shea, June 1, 1929 at St. James Church, Philadelphia by Rev. Edward P. Burke. Certificate No. 573531

DEATHS

James S. Crunkleton d. Nov 9, 1902, aged 66 years, 3 months and 4 days.

Rebecca B. Crunkleton d. Sep 18, 1920, aged 79 years, 11 months and 21 days.

Williams Port October 6, 1815
John Herr's Book
Herr Records

John Herr m. Catharine Boroff Aug 28, 1810 by the Revern Jonathan Rahauser of Hagerstown. Lived together in a married state Eleven years and Eleven days.

John Herr m. Sarah Boroff Oct 23, 1823.

George Albert m. Mary Ann Herr Tuesday Nov 25, 1828, by the Rev. Jno. Winder.

James W. Reynolds m. Susanna Herr on Thursday Oct 16, 1834 by the Rev. Mr. T. (or L.) W. Harkey.

Augustus C. Martin m. Eliza Herr on Thursday Sep 5, 1839 by the Rev. C. Startzman.

John P. Herr m. Sarah H. Fitzpatrick of Lexington, Lafayette County, Missouri on Tuesday Oct 13, 1840.

Henry G. Herr m. Catharine R. Jennings of Jennings County, Indiana, Apr 22, 1849.

Henry C. Herr m. Rebecca H. Roberts July 10, 1851. State of Indiana.

William L. Herr m. Columbia A. Chambers Tuesday Jan 10, 1854 by the Rev. A. H. Spilman at Culpeper C(ourt) H(ouse), Virginia.

Thomas W. Norris m. Isabella Herr in the Lutheran Church, Shepherdstown, Jefferson County, West Va. on Wednesday, Nov 21, 1877 by the Rev. R. C. Holland.

On a loose page in the Herr Bible: "Hymn Prepared for, and sung at a Confirmation, Held in the German Lutheran Church, Hagerstown May, 1820, Benjamin Kurtz, V.D.M." Certificate for Sally Boroff.

BIRTHS

John Herr b. Nov 29, 1789 and my wife Catharine Herr b. July 6, 1790, and my wife Sarah Herr b. Aug 3, 1797.

Children of Henry C. and Catherine Herr: Margaret R. and Sarah E. Herr were b. Sep 6, 1850.

The children of John and Catherine (Boroff) Herr:

1- Mary Ann Herr b. Thursday July 11, 1811 and was bapt. Aug 11, 1811 by the (Christian) Revern Jonathan Rahauser in Hagerstown.

2- Elizabeth Herr b. Friday Apr 9, 1813 and was bapt. on May 23, 1813 by the Christian Revern W. Houffman in Chambersburg.

3- Susanna Herr b. Monday Sep 12, 1814 and was bapt. (Christian) on Nov 27, 1814 by the Reveren Jonathan Rahauser of Hagerstown.

4- Eleanor and Eliza Herr b. Tuesday, March 19, 1816 and were bapt. (Christian) on Aug 4, 1816 by the Rev. Benjamin Kurtz in Hagerstown.

5-John Peter Herr b. Monday Apr 6, 1818 and was bapt. May 11, 1818.

6- George Washington Herr b. Tuesday Dec 21, 1819 and was bapt. Jan 9, 1820 by the Rev. James R. Reily of Hagerstown.

7-A dau. Still born on Friday morning about 2 o'clock Sep 7, 1821.

The Children of John and Sarah Herr

1- William La Fayette Herr b. Friday Dec 24, 1824 and was bapt. by the Rev. J. R. Reily on Jan 23, 1825.

2- Henry Clay Herr b. Sunday May 21, 1826 and was bapt. by the Rev. Isaac Kellar Oct 25, 1826.

3- Henrietta Catharine Herr b. Thursday, Sep 20, 1827 and was bapt. Apr 2, 1828 by the Rev. John Winter of Williamsport.

4- Edward Green Williams Herr b. Monday Mar 30, 1829 and was bapt. Jan 12, 1830 by the Rev. John Winter of Williamsport.

5- Ann William Herr b. Friday Sep 3, 1830 and was bapt. May 23, 1831 by the Rev. John Winter of Williamsport.

6- Samuel Horatio Herr b. Thursday June 28, 1832 and was bapt. Nov 7, 1832 by the Rev. John Winter of Williamsport.

7- Sarah Jane Herr b. Sunday, Jan 19, 1834 and was bapt. Mar 23, 1835 by the Rev. Isaac Keller of Williamsport.

8- Isabella Herr b. Sunday, Jan 17, 1836 and was bapt. Apr 27, 1838 by the Rev. John Winter of Williamsport.

9- Elizabeth Beecher Herr b. Sunday, Sep 16, 1838 at one o'clock a.m. and was bapt. June 9, 1841 by the Rev. Christian Startzman of WmsPort.

DEATHS

Elizabeth Beecher Herr Entler d. Nov 25, 1920 at 7 P.M. Thursday, in Los Angeles, California.

Elizabeth Herr d. in Chambersburg on Tuesday, Feb 1, 1814, her age was 9 months and 23 days.

My wife, Catharine Herr d. in Wmsport on Saturday evening, ten minutes before five o'clock, Sep 8, 1821, her age was 31 years, 2 months, 2 days.

Elenora Herr d. in Williamsport on Monday night at half after nine o'clock, Feb 6, 1837, her age was 20 years, 10 months, 18 days.

Susanna Reynolds, wife of James W. (or M.) Reynolds, d. in Fredericktown on Sunday, Aug 4, 1839, her age was 24 years, 10 months and 23 days.

James W. Reynolds d. July 5, 1849.

My Mother, Susanna Herr d. in Greencastle on Sunday morning about 6 o'clock, Mar 14, 1841. Her age was 79 years, 2 months, 2 days.

Mary Ann Albert, wife of George Albert d. in Williamsport on Wednesday Apr 24, 1844, her age was 32 years, 9 months, 13 days.

My father John P. Herr d. in Greencastle on Monday May 26, 1845 at 2 o'clock p.m., his age is 87 years, 9 months, 8 days.

Eliza Marten, wife of A. C. Marten d. in Williamsport on Friday, Feb 10, 1854 at 2 o'clock p.m., her age was 27 years, 10 months, 23 days.

John Herr d. in Williamsport on Monday night Jan 29, 1855 at 10 o'clock, his age was 65 years and 2 months.

Our brother, Samuel Horatio Herr d. in St. Louis Apr 12, 1870 at 5 o'clock a.m. His age was 37 years, 9 months, 14 days.

Our Mother, Sarah Herr d. in Williamsport, Md. on Friday at half past two o'clock p.m. Apr 29, 1870. Her age was 72 years, 8 months and 26 days.

Daiel (Daniel) W. Cyester, husband of Henrietta Cyester, d. May 4, 1874 aged 46 years.

Henrietta Catharine Herr Cyester d. in Williamsport, Md. on Monday, Oct 31, 1904. Her age 77 years, 1 month, 13 days.

William L. Herr d. in Staunton, Va. on Monday, Nov 19, 1894, his age was 69 years, 10 months, 25 days.

Edward G. W. Herr d. in Jefferson Co., West Va. on Friday Mar 8, 1901. His age was 71 years, 11 months, 8 days.

Isabella Norris, wife of T. W. Norris, d. in Washington, D.C. on Wednesday Nov 6, 1901 at 6 o'clock p.m. Her age was 65 years, 9 months, 19 days.

William Osbourn, husband of Sarah Jane Osbourn d. in Shenandoah Co., Va. June 8, 1901 aged 66 years.

Samuel Lefever, husband of Ann W. Lefever, d. Feb 7, 1904 aged 89 years.

Ann W. Lefever d. Nov 13, 1905 - 75 years.

Sarah Jane Osbourne d. Feb 4, 1919 age 85 years. Died at Leetown, W.Va.

(The Herr Bible is now in possession of Mr. Samuel Lefever of Hagerstown, Md.)

Wolf Bible Records

"These Wolfs did not come to Washington County, Md. until 1793. Jacob and John came first (see Wolf deeds of Wash. Co.) Records from the Wolf Bible, near Manor Church."

Issue of Jacob Wolf and Chaterina Zug b. 1760 of Jacob.

1. Elizabeth Wolf b. Aug 15, 1782 m. Jacob Rowland.

2. Susanna Wolf b. Oct 11, 1784 m. George Royer.

3. John Wolf b. Aug 16, 1786 m. Elizabeth Middlekauff, sister of David Wolf's wife.

4. Catherine Wolf b. Dec 23, 1788 m. David Rinehart.

5. Jacob Wolf b. June 17, 1791.

6. David Wolf b. Aug 6, 1793 m. Susanna(?) Middlekauff.

7. Mary Wolf b. Mar 26, 1796 m. John Slifer (See records of Fahrney Church, p. 333).

8. Barbara Wolf b June 8, 1811 d. unmarried.

Children of David Wolf and Susanna Middlekauff:

(Fahrney Church records, p. 333 under Daniel Wolf)

1. Elizabeth and Mary Wolf, b. July 30, 1817.

2. Catherine b. June 29, 1819.

3. David b. Apr 4, 1821.

4. Susanna Wolf b. May 5, 1823.

5. Daniel Wolf b. August 11, 1825 m. Anna Maria Rowland p. 334.

6. John Wolf b. Nov 15, 1827.

7. Sarah Wolf b. Apr 5, 1831.

8. Margaret Wolf b. July 13, 1833.

9. Samuel Wolf b. July 11, 1836.

Bible Records of George C. Bowman, Jr.

(Owned by Mrs. Lauran Benchoff, Smithsburg, Md. 1870)

George Bowman b. Nov 8, 1841 or (1847)

Susanah Bowman b. Jul 27, 1833

Joseph Bowman b. June 27, 1843

Henry Bowman b. 1845

George Bowman b. Mar 10, 1804

George Bowman, Jr. m. Cathrine McAfee Aug 5, 1830

John Bowman, son of Geo. Bowman and Cathrine McAfee Bowman b. May 29, 183? probably 1835 illegible

Susannah Bowman b. July 27, (1833)

John Bowman, son of Geo. Bowman and Cathrine McAfee b. May 29, 1831

Maria Bowman b. Dec 14, 1836

David Bowman b. Feb 6, 1838

Jane Bowman Miner, sister of Charles Bowman had dau. Mammie Miner who m. Anthony Eugene Rudisill. Lydia Miner Rudisill had son George Rudisill.

Family Records of the L. B. Brenner Family

Lucien Bonaparte Brenner b. Nov 27, 1838, d. Oct 23, 1920, aged 81 years.

Wife-Mary Catherine Fiery b. Apr 2, 1841, d. Oct 15, 1921, m. Dec 23, 1862.

Children:
1. Edgar Irving Brenner b. Aug 15, 1865, d. Dec 21 1886 in his 21st year - drowned while a Seminarian at Yale University, New Haven, Conn. Poet.
2. Walter Dallas Brenner b. May 19, 1868, d. Dec 29, 1937 m. Carrie Donaldson.
3. Edith Grace Brenner b. Nov 25, 1870, d. Aug 11, 1959 m. Harry Lyday Rinehart, teacher.
4. Alice Belle Brenner b. Feb 24, 1873. d. June 9, 1965 m. Lancelot Jacques.
5. Effie Kate Brenner b. Aug 31, 1875, d. Feb 23, 1953 m. Hubert Koontz.
6. Lula Emma Brenner b. June 28, 1878, d. Oct 23, 1880.
7. Florence Viola Brenner b. Aug 24, 1880, d. Apr 21, 1970, m. Joseph Sitler.
8. Bertha Barbara Brenner b. Sep 25, 1883, d. July 25, 1952 m. Dr. Maurice Daniel Kefauver.

Schleigh Bible Records

Jacob Brown Schleigh b. Aug 20, 1814, d. Apr 28, 1874

Sarah Ann Kraemer (Ragan) Schleigh b. ---, d. Dec 25, 1877, buried Zion Reformed Cemetery, Hagerstown, Md.

Their Children:
1. Martha Jane Schleigh b. May 24, 1846, d. Feb 24, 1912, m. Thomas A. Nock b. June 6, 1837, d. Mar 23, 1918.

2. Daniel F. Schleigh (b. Apr 4, 1849, d. Oct 28, 1879), m. Laura V. Titlow (b. May 18, 1850, d. Aug 25, 1926), dau. of Jacob D. and Eleanor Elkins Titlow of Frederick, Md. Buried Mt. Olivet Cem. Frederick.

3. Lucretia Ann Schleigh (b. Apr 17, 1852, d. Nov 24, 1925) m. Calvin B. Thurston (b. Jan 5, 1851, d. Dec 16, 1904).

4. Charles McGill Schleigh (b. Nov 6, 1858, d. Nov 30, 1910) m. Fannie May Hawkins (b. Dec 23, 1868, d. Dec 6, 1955).

5. Margaret Schleigh (b. 1852-1858, d. Mar 5, 1940) m. Rev. George H. Nock (d. Jul 13, 1911).

All buried in Rose Hill, Hagerstown, Md.

6. Her son by marriage to Ragan: Jonathan H. Ragan of Illinois.

Holy Bible of Ann Sarina Geiser Feb 12, 1859.
Records of Geiser Family Bible

David Geiser b. June 30, 1832 and Ann Sarina Browning b. Jul 18, 1836 m. June 23, 1858.

Father b. on Geiser Homestead, Smithsburg, Md., Mother b. Montgomery Co., Md. near Monrovey (Monrovia) dau. of Silas and Mary Browning.

BIRTHS

Sarah Lourenne Geiser b. Mar 23 1859

David Peter Geiser b. June 30, 1867

Emma Catherine Geiser b. Apr 4, 1862

Mary Lucinda Geiser b. Nov 13, 1868

Samuel Martin Geiser b. Sep 10, 1868

John Silas Geiser b. Mar 29, 1870

Nancy May Geiser b. Aug 1, 1871

Elizabeth Ann Geiser b. Feb 6, 1873

Aaron David Geiser b. July 24, 1874

William Elmer Geiser b. Nov 24, 1875

Jesse Geiser b. July 1, 1879

Infant son b. May 7, (or 1st) 1882

DEATHS

William E. Geiser d. July 8, 1876

Infant son d. May 2, 1882

Our Father, David Geiser d. Feb 6, 1885

Our Brother, Samuel M. Geiser Aug 30, 1889

Our Mother, Ann Sarina Geiser d. Nov 6, 1911

Aaron David Geiser d. Oct 31, 1948

Our Brother, David P. Geiser d. Jan 5, 1914

Elizabeth Ann Geiser d. May 5, 1944 (Chymaus)

Jesse E. Geiser d. Aug 16, 1955

Nancy May Geiser d. Apr 6, 1945

Emma Catherine Geiser Byers d. Jul 2, 1928

Mary Lucinda Geiser Sellers d. 1896

Sarah Lourena Geiser Zuck d. Aug 3, 1918

John Silas Geiser d. Nov, 1934

From a clipping: "Anna Sarina, widow of the late David Geiser b. at Monrovia, Montgomery Co, Md. died Nov. 6, 1911 aged 73 at Waynesboro, Pa. Leaves four sons and four daughters, including J. S. Geiser, a minister of Baltimore, Md."

From a sheet of paper found in Family Bible

[Apparently this page showed the ages of each person named theron on December 27, 1884.]

David Geiser b. 1832-6-30; 1884-12-27

Ann S. Geiser b. 1838-7-18; 1884-12-27

Sarah L. Geiser b. 1859-3-23; 1884-12-27

Emma C. Geiser b. 1862-4-4, 1884-12-27

Mary L. Geiser b. 1864-11-13

Daniel P. Geiser b. 1867-6-30

Samuel M. Geiser b. 1868-9-10

J. S. Geiser b. 1870-3-25

Nancy M. Geiser b. 1871-8-1

E. A. Geiser b. 1873-1-6

Aaron D. Geiser b. 1874-7-24

William E. Geiser b. 1875-11-24

Jesse E. Geiser b. 1879-7-1

Family of Joseph S. Horst

Joseph S. Horst of Franklin Co., Pa. and Anna M. Shindle of Franklin Co., Pa. were m. Sep 7, 1876 at Parsonage of John Shank.

Witnesses: Abram Hollinger and Henry Hykes. [This is a photocopy of marriage certificate.]

BIRTHS

Joseph S. Horst b. Sep 21, 1851

Anna Maria Horst b. Oct 4, 1857

Mintie May Horst b. Dec 21, 1877

Clinton Horst b. Apr 5, 1879

Clare Rebecca Horst b. Dec 30, 1880

Anna Florence Horst b. Sep 14, 1882

Edna Catherine Horst b. Dec 18, 1895

MARRIAGES

Clara Rebecca Horst m. Samuel H. Petre Dec 19, 1901

Anna Florence Horst m. John Calvin Meyers Dec 20, 1906

Mintie Mae Horst m. Jacob Dunkleberger Nov 17, 1909

DEATHS

Clinton (Hearst) Horst d. Aug 30, 1888

Joseph S. Horst d. May 30, 1910

Anna Florence Meyers d. Oct 14, 1923

Anna M. (Shindle) Horst d. July 2, 1933

Jacob Dunkelberger d. Mar 3, 1953

John Calvin Meyers d. Feb 9, 1958

Mintie May Dunkleberger d. May 27, 1961

Samuel Horst Petre d. Mar 28, 1966

Clara Rebecca Petre d. July 9, 1971 aged 90 years

Edna Catherine Horst d. July 11, 1973 aged 77 years

Notes from Mary Bester Kneisley Bowman (Mrs. Henry D.) From a Letter of Recommendation now in possession of Susan Bester, the German original.

Great-grand father was Wilhelm Bester, b. in Kassel, son of Eberhard Bester of Schonfeld;

Studied in Electoral hot houses (landscape gardening) horticultural in Holland 1818 - 1821.

His mother's maiden name was Shillhaus - her two brothers were in the seed business - his father had greenhouses in Schoenfeld, Holland.

King William sent grand father Bester to Kaiser Wilhelm to landscape gardens like the Hanging Gardens of Babylon.

Elizabeth Dorothea Marth (or Morth) was grandmother Bester (wife of Wilhelm) b. in Wurthemberg - Interterkheim, Stuttgart. His sister was Christine Burner.

Children of Wilhelm and Elizabeth Bester

1. William

    Children: Mary, Renie, Daisy (Kneisley), son Harry

2. Harry m.

    Children: Henry, Fred, Clara

3. ---- m. Danzer

Mary Kneisley Bowman was the dau. of Daisy Bester and Dr. Kneisley. Their only child, Mary m. Dr. Harry Bowman.

Her grandmother Kneisley was an Anderson, dau. of Black whose mother was a Grove.

Grandmother Grove was raised by her aunt and uncle, the Clowers (Clawers or Clamers). She inherited their house and lived in it all of her life.

Grandmother's (Grove) sister m. a Bowman another, an Ott.

This family lived in Virginia.

Ziegler Bible

MARRIAGES

George S. Zeigler and Susann Wolfersberger m. Apr 13, 1848.

Henry Barnhard m. Susan Zeigler Nov 14, 1861.

Levi B. Wolfinger m. Annie M. C. Zeigler Oct 30, 1879 by Rev Dr. J. W. Santee.

Charles B. Wolfinger m. Mary Alice Wolfinger Aug 24, 1893 by Rev. C. A. Santee.

BIRTHS

George S. Zeigler b. Sep 27, 1826

Susanna Wolfensberger b. Apr 25, 1833

Henry Barnhart b. Dec 22, 1822

Mary Allas Zeigler b. Nov 5, 1850

Anna Margaret Carl(?) Zeigler b. Dec 11, 1852

Jacob Alonza Ziegler b. Oct 20, 1854

Abigail Zeigler b. Oct 23, 1856

Emma Susan Barnhart b. July 29, 1862

DEATHS

Henry Barnhart d. Nov 21, 1862

George Zeigler d. Aug 4, 1857

Susan Zeigler Barnhart d. Mar 5, 1907 aged 74 years

Emma Susan (Barnhart) Mentzer d. June 12, 1922

Mary A. Wolfinger d. Dec 12, 1926

Abigail Ziegler d. Dec 25, 1932 Christmas morn

Jacob A. Ziegler d. Aug 28, 1935 aged 80 years

From Family Bible of Daniel Wolf

Daniel Wolf m. Ann Maria Rowland Oct 15, 1850

William R. Wolf m. Susan Jane Young Dec 23, 1879

Samuel H. Neikirk m. Nancy Catharine Wolf Dec 13, 1881

John Shively Wolf m. Mary Ellen Yonty Jan 14, 1885

Charles Thomas Mumma m. Susan Isabell Wolf Jan 20, 1890

Joseph Daniel Wolf m. Edna C. Long Dec 5, 1894

Ellen M. Wolf m. Aaron Mullendore Dec 14, 1886

BIRTHS

David Wolf b. Aug 6, 1793

Susan Wolf b. Mar 15, 1798

Daniel Wolf b. Aug 11, 1823 (or 1827)

Ann Maria Rowland b. Dec 11, 1828

Emma Cora Wolf b. Oct 10, 1851

William Rowland Wolf b. Sep 11, 1853

Nancy Catherine Wolf b. Dec 27, 1856

Mary Wolf b. Nov 29, 1858

John Shively Wolf b. Jan 2, 1861

Sarah Jane Wolf b. Oct 24, 1862

Ellen M. Wolf b. Dec 20, 1864

Susan Isabel Wolf b. Aug 20, 1866

Bettie Laura Wolf b. June 8, 1868

Joseph Daniel Wolf b. July 11, 1870

Fanny May Wolf b. Nov 27, 1873

Wilbur Wolf Mumma b. Feb 11, 1900

Samuel Henry Neikirk d. Aug 22, 1926 aged 71 years, 4 days

Charles Thomas Mumma d. Nov 16, 1926, aged 60 years, 8 months, 6 days

Isabell Lannia Wolf d. June 3, 1909

DEATHS

Susan Wolf d. Oct 10, 1839 aged 41 years, 6 months, 1 day

David Wolf d. Apr 17, 1845 aged 52 years, 8 months, 11 days

Sarah Jane Wolf d. July 9, 1864 aged 1 year, 8 months, 15 days

Ellen M. Mullendore d. Feb 4, 1888, 23 years, 1 month, 14 days

Daniel Wolf d. Aug 16, 1899, aged 74 years, 5 days

Emma Mary Wolf d. Oct 21, 1912 aged 83 years, 10 months, 2 days

Fannie May Wolf d. May 20, 1903 aged 29 years, 5 months, 23 days

Wilbur Wolf Mumma d. Aug 15, 1911, aged 14 years, 6 months, 4 days

Nannie C. Neikirk d. May 7, 1926, aged 70 years, 4 months, 17 days

Susan Isabell Mumma d. July 11, 1926 aged 59 years, 10 months, 11 days

Emma Cora Wolf d. June 17, 1929 aged 77 years, 8 months, 7 days

William Rowland Wolf d. Mar 4, 1932 aged 78 years, 5 months, 22 days

Mary Wolf d. June 13, 1933 aged 74 years, 6 months, 14 days

Bettie Laura Wolfe d. Oct 4, 1936 aged 68 years, 4 months, 26 days

Joe Wolf d. March 31, 1938

Edna Catherine Wolfe d. Sep 21, 1939 aged 66 years, Thursday at Hospital

Zug (Zuch, Zook) Records

Children of the Original Jacob Zug

1. Chaterina Zug b. Apr 27, 1760 m. Jacob Wolf
2. Johannes Zug b. Sep 20, 1763
3. Elizabeth Zug b. Feb 22, 1765
4. Susana Zug b. Sep 13, 1766
5. Salomna Zug b. Apr 16, 1769
6. Maria Zug b. July 19, 1773
7. Jacob Zug b. Aug 15, 1775
8. David Zug b. Apr 27, 1778

Children of Jacob Zug b. Aug 15, 1775 d. 1823 and Magdaline Emmet Bible Record

John Zug b. Jan 22, 1799, 9 a.m.
Cadrinah Zug, dau. b. May 16, 1800
Jacob son b. May 9, 1802
David son b. Sep 9, 1804
Daniel son b. Nov 14, 1809
Anna dau. b. Jan 24, 1811
Susanna dau. b. Mar 14, 1813
Magdalina dau. b. Feb 9, 1815
Elizabeth dau. b. Aug 11, 1816
Sarah dau. b. Mar 5, 1819

Jacob Zug's Bible Record

John Zug b. 1799 m. Nancy Anna Hawbaker

Catherine Zug b. 1800 m. William Engle (Angle)

Jacob Zug b. 1802 m. Susan

David Zug b. 1804 m. Elizabeth Negley

Daniel Zug b. 1809 m. Hannah Butterbaugh

Anna Zug b. 1811 m. Benjamin Elliott

Susanna Zug b. 1813 m. David Cushwa

Magdalina Zug b. 1815 m. John T. Brewer

Elizabeth Zug b. 1816 m. John Wolff

Sarah Zug b. 1819 m. John Carnes

From Wolf Bible, near Manor Church, the issue of Jacob Wolf and Catherine Zug (b. Apr 27, 1760) dau. of Jacob Zug:

Elizabeth Wolf b. Aug 15, 1782 m. Jacob Rowland.
Susanna Wolf b. Oct 11, 1784 m. George Royer.
John Wolf b. Aug 16, 1786 m. Elizabeth Middlekauff, sister of David's wife.
Catherine Wolf b. Dec 23, 1788 m. David Rinehart.
Jacob Wolf b. Jan 17, 1791.

Catherine Wolf b. Dec 23, 1788 m. David Rinehart.

Jacob Wolf b. Jan 17, 1791.

David Wolf b. Aug 6, 1793 m. Susanna (?) Middlekauff.

Mary Wolf b. Mar 26, 1796 m. John Slifer (Fahrney Church records p. 333).

Barbara Wolf b. June 8, 1811 d. unmarried.

Children of David and Susanna (Middlekauff) Wolf from records of Fahrney's Church p. 333

Elizabeth Wolf b. July 30, 1817

Mary Wolf b. July 30, 1817

Catherine Wolf b. June 29, 1819

David Wolf b. Apr 4, 1821

Susanna Wolf b. May 5, 1823

Daniel Wolf b. Aug 11, 1825

John Wolf b. Nov 15, 1827

Sarah Wolf b. Apr 5, 1831

Margaret Wolf b. July 13, 1833

Samuel Wolf b. July 11, 1836

Marriages from the Wolf Family Bible

Daniel Wolf m. Ann Maria Rowland Oct 15, 1850

William R. Wolf m. Susan Jane Young Dec 23, 1879

Samuel H. Neikirk m. Nancy Catherine Wolf Dec 13, 1881

John Shively Wolf m. Mary Elln Yourtey Jan 24, 1885

Chas. Thos. Mumma m. Susan Isabell Wolf m. Jan 20, 1890

Joseph Daniel Wolf m. Edna C. Long Dec 5, 1894

Ellen M. Wolf m. Aaron Mullendore Dec 14, 1886

"Copy of records which were apparently in a Family Bible which has not been located."

Philomena A. Althoff b. Apr 20, 1886 at 10 o'clock in the evening

Carrie's father - William A. Althoff b. May 17, 1827 at 12 o'clock midnight; d. Aug 14, 1904 age 77 years, 6 months, 2 days

Carrie's mother - Mary J. Althoff b. June 6, 1842; d. Jan 8, 1899 age 56 years, 7 months, 2 days

William A. Althoff and Mary J. Warthen m. Apr 16, 1861 in Mt. St. Mary's Church, Emmitsburg, Md.

Carrie's Father's Family (and Grandma Flautts)

John M. Althoff b. June 28, 1814 at 6 o'clock in the evening

Ann C. Althoff b. Sep 1, 1816 at 10 o'clock in the evening

Henry Jerome Althoff b. Feb 17, 1819 at 2 o'clock in the morning

Grandma and Grandpa Flautt m. in Emmitsburg, Md. Mt. St. Mary's Church

Her bro's (Carrie's): John, Henry, William, Frank, Luke, Felix, Pius (7 boys, 1 girl

William H. Althoff b. Feb 11, 1863 at 3 o'clock in the morning

Joseph F. Althoff b. Feb 22, 1865

George F. Althoff b. May 3, 1867, at 11 o'clock in the evening

Catherine C. Althoff b. Nov 16, 1869, at 3 in the morning

Mary A. Althoff b. Mar 20, 1872, at 2 in the morning

Michael A. Althoff b. Oct 7, 1875, at 2 in the morning

John P. Althoff b. Feb 1, 1878, at 12 noon

Charles F. Althoff b. Dec 23, 1879, 5 o'clock in the morning

Peter Pius Althoff b. Dec 8, 1821 at 8 o'clock in the morning

James F. Althoff b. Nov 6, 1824 at 7 o'clock in the morning

William A. Althoff b. May 17, 1827 at 12 o'clock midnight

Joseph A. Althoff b. Aug 6, 1830 at 11 o'clock in the evening

Felix M. Althoff b. Apr 19, 1835 at 9 o'clock in the morning

DEATHS (of Carries' Father's Family

Mother-Catherine Althoff d. June 22, 1853, age 62 years, 9 months, 29 days

Father-Henry Althoff d. Oct 7, 1853, age 73 years, 9 months, 23 days

Bro.-Henry J. Althoff d. Sep 22, 1830, age 19 years, 7 months, 5 days

Bro.- James F. Althoff d. Sep 2, 1863, age 38 years, 9 months, 28 days

Sister-Ann C. Flautt d. Jan 10, 1897 age 80 years, 4 months, 10 days

Bro.-John M. Althoff d. Aug 26, 1899 age 85 years, 28 days

My grandfather and grandmother

Henry Althoff
Catherine Althoff
and my father's brother - Uncle Henry Althoff
Sister Editha Althoff
Cousin Emma Ohmer
Cousin Lillie Grinner

MISCELLANEOUS RECORDS

On Microfilm (Reel No. BP 8, Maryland State Department of Health, Bureau of Vital Statistics.

John Wesley Barnes b. Aug 18, 1865

Alice Rebecca Barnes b. Feb 1st 1872

Raymond Wesley Barnes b. March 13, 1893

Millard Omer Barnes b. Oct 8, 1894

Norman Oliver Barnes b. Nov 23, 1895

Annie Catharine Barnes b. Oct 23, 1898

Walter Samuel Barnes b. Jan 18, 1900

Carl Scott Barnes b. Sep 9, 1901

Alvin Roscoe Barnes b. Feb 26, 1904

Earl Atte [Atle?] Barnes b. Feb 25, 1906

Ethel Naomie Barnes b. Oct 18, 1907

John Edwin Barnes b. Aug 18, 1909

Ralph Moats Barnes b.Aug 29, 1911

Harry M. Ditmer b. March 22, 1894

Fannie Ditmer b. May 15, 1898

Claude Edward Ditmer b. Jan 1915; d. Dec 23, 1916, age 1 year, 11 mos., 22 days

Johny Albert Ditmer b. July 17, 1917

Dorothy Marie Ditmer b. June 29, 1919

Helen Louise Ditmer b. Aug 26, 1922

Betty Jane Ditmer b. June 8, 1927

BUTLER,
Temperance, 55
Temperance Eliza, 54
BUTTERBAUGH,
Hannah, 95
BYERS,
Elizabeth Gardner, 24
Emma Catherine
Geiser, 89

-C-
CALENDER,
S. N., 79
CARNER,
Ed, 28
CARNES,
John, 95
CARNEY,
Bess, 28
CARTER,
George B., 29
Richard B., 29
Susan Funk, 29
CASTLE,
E. B. C., 15
CHAMBERS,
Columbia A., 83
CHUSING,
Edmund, 30
CHYMAUS,
Elizabeth Ann, 89
CLAMERS,
---, 92

CLARK,
Chester, 11
David, 26
CLAWERS,
---, 92
CLOWERS,
---, 92
COBBREGHT,
Rev., 59
CONLEY,
Delva, 67
William Charles, 54
COOKE,
Addison Barnwell, 35, 36, 37
J. Addison, 36
Mary Sams, 36
Mary Wilson, 36
COOPER,
Geary A., 7, 32, 33, 46, 47
Susie Frey, 7
Susie Frye, 33, 47
COPPER,
---, 33
CORCORAN,
Ann, 28
COULDRAN,
Agnes, 28
Angie, 28
Annie, 28
Jean, 28
Judge, 28
Tom, 28

COURTNEY,
Austin M., 24
CRABB,
Margaret, 16
CRADDOCK,
Ellen, 29
John, 29
Margaret, 29
Sarah Ann, 29
CRAFT,
---, 14
CRAIG,
Florence V., 79
CRAMPHIN,
Ruth, 16
Thomas, 16
CRAMPTON,
Eli, 42
CRAWLEY,
Louise, 28
CREAGER,
Bob, 56
CRUNKLETON,
Daisy Agnes, 82
Dorothy, 81
George W., 81, 82
James S., 81, 82
Rebecca B., 82
CULBERTSON,
D., 3
Mary E., 1, 26
CUNNINGHAM,
Mary Louise, 41

CUSHWA,
David, 95
CYESTER,
Daiel W., 85
Daniel W., 85
Henrietta, 85
Henrietta Catharine
Herr, 85

-D-
DANZER,
---, 91
DAVIS,
Annie, 29
Catharine W., 17
Ellen, 29
George, 29
Joe, 29
William, 29
DELANY,
John, 81
DICK,
Josie E., 73
DITMER,
Betty Jane, 99
Claude Edward, 99
Dorothy Marie, 99
Fanny, 98
Harry M., 98
Helen Louise, 99
Johny Albert, 99
DONALDSON,
Carrie, 87

DOUB,
Abner, 40
Catharine, 40
Catherine, 29
Charles, 40
Daisy D., 40
Edward C., 39, 40
Harry G., 40
Jennie F., 40
Mollie R., 40
Richard, 39
William D., 40
DUNKLEBERGER,
Jacob, 90
Mintie May, 91
DUNN,
Alice Margret, 60
Amelia Jane, 60
Arabell, 60
Catherine, 60
Clyde Riley, 73, 74
Daniel, 59, 60
E., 59
Edwin Preston, 60
Elizabeth, 60
Elizabeth Ellen, 60
John, 73
John Daniel, 73
John P., 60
Laura V., 73, 74
Mary Catherine, 60
W. H., 73
William H., 73
William Hollen, 60

-E-
EARNSHAW,
Meda Herbert, 23
Meta Herbert, 23
EDMONDS,
George H., 29
George Henry, 29
Margaret, 29
Marie Funk, 29
Roger T., 29
EHLEN,
Amelia Louise, 68
EICHELBERGER,
Barbara, 7
Theobold, 7
ELLIOTT,
Benjamin, 95
EMMET,
Magdaline, 95
ENGLE,
William, 95
ENSMINGER,
R. W., 73
ETZLER,
Louise C., 56
EVANS,
Joshua, 78

-F-
FAGUE,
Catharine, 8
Edward E., 8
John, 8

HAMMACKER,
  Adam, 12
  Anna, 12
  Daniel, 12
  David, 12
  Ephriam, 12
  John Hubert, 12
  Maria, 12
  Peter, 12
  Samuel, 12
  Solomon, 12
  Sophia, 12
HAMMAKER,
  Adam, 22
  Amanda, 22
  Anna, 13, 20, 21, 22
  Daniel, 22
  Ella, 22
  Ephraim, 22
  Lizzie, 22
  Maria, 22
  Mary, 21, 22
  Peter, 20, 22
  Samuel, 22
  Solomon, 22
  Sophia, 22
  Stewart, 22
HAMMOND,
  Catharine, 69
HANNA,
  John, 25, 26, 37
  Margaretta, 37, 38
  Mary, 25, 37

HARBAUGH,
  Jacob, 25
HARKEY,
  L. W., 82
  T. W., 82
HARSHMAN,
  Mary Virginia, 63
HARTLE,
  Bessie Lee, 63
HARTLEY,
  Thomas A., 61
HAUSE,
  Sarah, 43
HAWBAKER,
  Nancy Anna, 95
HAWKEN,
  Bertie Imo, 23
HAWKINS,
  Fannie May, 88
HAYMAN,
  E. T., 37
  Edgar, 38
  Edgar T., 24, 25
  Edgar Thomas, 35, 36, 37
  Elijah R., 36
  Elijah Robert, 37
  Margaret Payne, 36, 37
  Margaretta, 24
HAZELHURST,
  Charles, 9
  Juliana Eleanor, 9
HAZLETT,
  Henry, 17

Mary Beall, 17
HEAGER,
  Jacob, 3
HEARD,
  Frank S., 29
  Kathryn M., 29
  Robert L., 29
HEARST,
  Clinton, 90
HEATON,
  Henry, 54
HEIMEL,
  Gottlieb Schmed, 78
  Gottlob, 78
  Justus, 78
  Katherine Wagner, 78
HERR,
  Ann William, 84
  Catharine, 83, 84
  Edward G. W., 85
  Edward Green Williams, 84
  Eleanor, 83
  Eleanora, 84
  Eliza, 82, 83
  Elizabeth, 83, 84
  Elizabeth Beecher, 84
  George Washington, 83
  Henrietta Catharine, 83
  Henry C., 82
  Henry Clay, 83
  Henry G., 82
  Isabella, 83, 84
  John, 82, 83, 85

HYKES,
  Henry, 90

-I-
IFERT,
  Daniel, 1
  John Henry, 1
  Susannah, 1
  William, 1
INGRAM,
  ---, 19
  Benjamin, 46
  Catharine, 46
  Catherine, 45
  Cynthia, 45
  Edith Huyett, 44, 45
  Edward, 44, 46
  Elizabeth, 46
  Elizabeth Florence, 44
  Henrietta, 45
  Jennie, 45
  John, 45, 46
  Joseph, 46
  Laura, 44
  Laura Virginia, 44
  Martha Ann, 44
  Martha E., 44
  Martha Ellen, 44
  Martha Huyett, 45
  Mary, 45
  Mary E., 45
  Mary Eliza, 44
  Rachel, 45, 46
  Rachel Catharine, 44, 45

Rachel Catherine, 44
Sarah, 45, 46
Susan, 45, 46
Tilly, 45
William, 45, 46

-J-
JACOBS,
  Elizabeth, 10, 49
  Virginia, 17
JACQUES,
  Lancelot, 87
JAMURE,
  J. S., 73
JENNINGS,
  Catharine R., 82
JOHNS,
  Thomas, 16
JOHNSON,
  A. J., 18
JONES,
  Daniel Martin, 51
  David Washington, 51
  Elizabeth, 52
  Elizabeth Bovey, 52
  Grandmother, 51
  Harrison Piper, 36
  J. R., 42
  Jacob Bovey, 51
  Jonathan, 51, 52
  Mary Wilson, 35
  Maryann, 51
  Maurice Hepburn, 35, 36
  Minnie A., 36

Simon, 51
Sophia Rosan, 51
William Bovey, 51

-K-
KAUFFMAN,
  Mary Ann, 6, 31, 46
KAYLOR,
  Harry, 70
  Isouria B., 66
  Isouria Bell, 65
  Isouria Bell Funk, 70, 71
  John W., 70
  Mary R., 70
KEFAUVER,
  Maurice Daniel, 87
KEIFAVER,
  Rev., 57
KELLAR,
  Isaac, 83
KELLER,
  George, 13
  Isaac, 84
KELLY,
  James W., 27
KENDLE,
  Vernie, 39, 40
KENDLE-KENDAL,
  John M., 40
KERFOOT,
  John B., 51
KETTERMAN,
  W. H., 57

RAHAUSER,
Fred., 57
Jonathan, 82
M., 57
RAHUASER,
Jonathan, 83
RANDOLPH,
Mary, 15
RANKIN,
Annie L., 3
Charles McLean
Knox, 27
Elizabeth, 2
Elizabeth Harriet, 27
Elizabeth K., 26
Elizabeth Knox, 3
Elizabeth W., 3
Elizabeth Watson, 2, 3, 27
Euphemia Mason Knox, 26
Helen Margaret Knox, 26
James C., 3
James Clark, 3
Jere C., 3
Jere Clark, 3
Jerry, 2, 3, 26
John, 26
John Knox, 26
Johnston, 2
Margaret Johnston, 3
Maria Louise, 3, 26
Martha Virginia, 27

Mary Helen Rinehart, 27
Mary Jane, 2, 3, 26
S. Johnston, 2, 3, 26
Samuel Johnston, 3, 27
Sarah Mary Knox, 26
REILLY,
Sarah, 73
REILY,
James R., 63, 83
James Ross, 59
RESH,
Elizabeth, 51
RESLEY,
Lydia, 80
REYNOLDS,
James M., 84
James W., 82, 84
Susanna, 84
RICH,
E. Albert, 31
RICHARDSON,
Clarence Rich., 20
Daniel S., 21
Daniel Stewart, 20
Elsio, 20
Francis Samuel, 20
H. J., 32, 46
Harry Earnest, 20
Herbert, 63
Howard, 20
Robert Howard, 20
Sallie, 21
Sallie J., 13, 20, 21
Scott, 20

Stewart, 20
William Alfred, 20
RIDENOUR,
Brayden, 65
Charles Edward, 1, 34
Daniel Newton, 1, 34
Daniel Nuton, 1, 34
Effa Jane, 1, 34
Emma Arbelan, 34
Emma Arbelon, 1
Etta, 34
George Melanchthon, 1, 34
Jacob, 1, 34
John Henry, 1, 34
Laura Etta, 1
Lewis Macelon, 34
Lewis Maclelon, 1
Mandy Catherine, 34
Mary Elen Rebecca, 34
Mary Ellen Rebecca, 1
Nandy Catharine, 1
Sarah Ann Elizabeth, 1, 34
Susanna, 34
Susannah, 1
RIDGELY,
Charles A., 27
RILEY,
Catherine, 73, 74
D. D., 73
Dennis DeWitt, 74
George W., 74
Jennie Belle, 73, 74
John, 73, 74

SCHAFF,
Philip, 39
SCHENI,
Kadiele, 76
SCHINDEL,
Andreas, 76
Anmaria, 76
Bertha Elizabeth, 72
Camilla F., 72
Camilla Frances, 72
Charlotte Esther, 72
Daniel, 76
Elizabeth, 59, 76
Etleina Efa, 76
George, 72, 75
Guy Roman, 72
Ida Camilla, 72
Jacob Henry, 76
Jonathan, 75
Julia Hade, 72
Louisa Sofia, 76
Ludwig, 72, 76
Norman E., 72
Oscar M., 72
Rebecka, 76
S. Milford, 72
Samuel, 72
Samuel Milford, 72
William, 76
SCHLEICH,
---, 57
An Leutrisha, 57
Ana Mary, 57
Christina Rebeka, 57
Jacob Brown, 57

John, 57
Thomas Eloia, 57
William, 57
SCHLEIGH,
Charles McGill, 88
Daniel F., 88
Daniel H., 57
Daniel Henry, 57
Ellen Alcinda, 58
Frederick Washington, 58
Jacob Brown, 87
John, 57
Josephen, 58
Lucretia Ann, 88
Lucretia Sophia, 58
Margaret, 88
Martha Jane, 87
Mary, 57
Mary Clorinda Rebeca, 58
Samuel Henry, 57
Sarah Ann Kraemer, 87
T. E., 57
SCHNEBLY,
Clarence Middlekauff, 79
Florence Craig, 79, 80
Gertrude E., 79
Gertrude Elizabeth, 78, 79
John, 80
John Bernard, 79, 80
Lewis Allen, 79

Lewis Resley, 79, 80
Lydia, 80
Lydia Resley, 80
Mary Catherine, 79, 80
Mary Louise, 79
Norman Goodrich, 79, 80
Samuel, 79, 80
Samuel R., 79
Samuel Resley, 79
SCHWARTZ,
Frank S., 74
Rachael S., 54
SCOTT,
E. H., 2, 3
George Marshall, 2
Mary, 23
Theresa, 23
William, 2
SELLERS,
Mary Lucinda Geiser, 89
SHANEBERGER,
Elizabeth Ann, 65
Elizabeth Ann Funk, 70
Lewis, 65
Lewis R., 70
SHANK,
John, 90
Susan, 22
SHEA,
Arthur Bernard, 81, 82
Daisy Crunkleton, 81

Elizabeth, 10, 11, 49, 50
Frederick, 10, 11, 50
Isabella, 11, 50
Margaret, 10, 51
Martin, 10, 49, 50
Mary, 10, 49, 50
Nancy, 10, 50
Peter, 10, 11, 50
Polly, 11, 50
Samuel, 10, 11, 49, 50
Susanna, 10
Susannah, 10, 50
William, 10
SPECKS,
Martin, 49
SPESSARD,
Anna Mary, 62
SPICKLER,
Nancy, 10, 49
SPIELMAN,
Mary T., 4
Mollie C., 61
SPILMAN,
A. H., 83
SPRECKER,
Charles, 40
STARTZMAN,
C., 82
Christian, 84
STATLER,
Kenneth Carl, 81
STEMBLE,
Mary, 57

STEPHEY,
Daniel, 21
Margaret, 13, 20
STEPHY,
Daniel, 13
STOCKSLAGER,
Susanna, 40
STONE,
Catherine, 73
Francis, 74
Margaret Ann, 74
Michael, 73
Sarah, 73
STORM,
Alice C., 52
F. E., 52
Frances E., 53
Frances M., 52
Frank E., 52
Harriet C., 52
Hattie, 52, 53, 54
John F., 52
Katie C., 52
Pauline S., 52
STOUFFER,
Elizabeth, 60
Frisby, 21
James L., 41
Rebecca, 10, 49
Rose Ann, 66
STOVER,
Daniel, 62
F. W., 73
Rose Ann, 66

STUMP,
Carry Wolf, 66
SWITZER,
Edward, 14
SWOPE,
Cecelia, 45
Elizabeth, 45
Ingram, 45
Laretta, 45
Mary, 45
Peter, 45
Samuel, 45

-T-
TAYLOR,
H. S., 19
Lilian Schindel, 74
TEMPLETON,
S. M., 54
THOMAS,
Catherine, 66
Cynthia, 66
Dora Geneva, 31
Elizabeth, 66
Jack, 66
Jacob, 66
John, 66
Rose Ann, 66
Susan, 66
Yoney, 66
THURSTON,
Calvin B., 88
TITLOW,
Eleanor Elkins, 88
Jacob D., 88

William Alforde, 7, 35
William Alfred, 35
William Geary, 35
WESTON,
Arthur Hazelhurst, 9
Benjamin Latrobe, 9
Cornelius, 9
Henry Bancroft, 9
Kate, 9
WHALEY,
Susie B., 32, 46
Susie Belle, 6, 32, 46
WIGDON,
Elenor, 19
WIGTON,
R. Benton, 19
WILHELM,
Kaiser, 91
WILLIAM,
King, 91
WILLIAMS,
Anna McDowell, 13, 14
Anna McPherson, 13, 14
Catharine L., 16
Catharine M., 14
Ella, 68
Helen Margaret, 13, 14
Laura, 16
Louise Jane, 13
Maria, 16
Mary Emma Berry, 13
Mary Holliday, 13

Otho, 13
Otho Holland, 16
Thomas Owen, 13, 14
Violetta, 13, 14
Virginia Washington, 13
WILSON,
Clyde H., 36
Clyde Huyett, 35, 36, 37
Elizabeth, 36, 37
Elizabeth Brewer, 37
Harriet Hillery, 37
John, 37
John H., 35, 36, 37
John Hamilton, 36, 37
Lancelot, 37
Lawrence, 37, 38
Margaretta, 37
Margaretta Helen, 35, 36
Margaretta O., 36, 37
Mary A., 36
Mary Adams, 35, 36, 37
Mary Elizabeth, 36
Rufus, 37
Rufus H., 35, 36
Rufus Hillary, 36
Rufus Hillery, 36, 37
WINDER,
John, 82
WINDERS,
Camilla, 72
Samuel, 72

WINDSER,
Edward, 4
Elizabeth F., 4
Elizabeth Frances, 5
Elizabeth Franley, 4
Emily C., 4
Fannie, 5
Fanny, 4
John H., 4, 5
Joseph, 5
Joseph R., 4
Newman, 4, 5
Norman, 4
Richard S., 4
Robert N., 4
WINDSOR,
Elizabeth F., 47
Elizabeth Frances, 48, 49
Emily C., 47
Fanny, 47, 48, 49
John H., 47, 48
Joseph P., 48
Joseph R., 47
Newman, 47, 48, 49
Richard L., 47
Robert N., 47
WINTER,
John, 83, 84
WINTERS,
Ann, 25
Ann V., 63
Ann Virginia, 63
WITHEROW,
Margaret, 1, 3, 26

Heritage Books by F. Edward Wright:

18th Century Records of the German Lutheran Church at Philadelphia, Pennsylvania (St. Michael's and Zion): Volume 1, Baptisms, 1745–1769
Robert L. Hess and F. Edward Wright

18th Century Records of the German Lutheran Church at Philadelphia, Pennsylvania (St. Michael's and Zion): Volume 2, Baptisms, 1770–1786
Translated by Robert L. Hess, Ph.D. Edited by F. Edward Wright

18th Century Records of the German Lutheran Church of Philadelphia, Pennsylvania (St. Michael's and Zion): Volume 3, Baptisms, 1787–1800
Translated by Robert L. Hess, Ph.D. Edited by F. Edward Wright

18th Century Records of the German Lutheran Church at Philadelphia, Pennsylvania (St. Michael's and Zion): Volume 4, Marriages and Confirmations
Robert L. Hess and F. Edward Wright

18th Century Records of the German Lutheran Church at Philadelphia, Pennsylvania (St. Michael's and Zion): Volume 5, Burials
Robert L. Hess and F. Edward Wright

Abstracts of Bucks County, Pennsylvania, Wills, 1685–1785

Abstracts of Cumberland County, Pennsylvania, Wills, 1750–1785

Abstracts of Cumberland County, Pennsylvania, Wills, 1785–1825

Abstracts of Philadelphia County, Pennsylvania, Wills:
Volumes: 1682–1726; 1726–1747; 1748–1763; 1763–1784; 1777–1790; 1790–1802; 1802–1809; 1810–1815; 1815–1819; and 1820–1825

Abstracts of South Central Pennsylvania, Newspapers, Volume 1, 1785–1790

Abstracts of South Central Pennsylvania, Newspapers, Volume 3, 1796–1800

Abstracts of the Newspapers of Georgetown and the Federal City, 1789–99

Abstracts of York County, Pennsylvania, Wills, 1749–1819

Adams County [Pennsylvania] Church Records of the 18th Century

Baltimore Directory of 1807

Berks County, Pennsylvania, Church Records of the 18th Century, Volumes 1–4

Bible Records of Washington County, Maryland

Bucks County, Pennsylvania, Church Records of the 17th and 18th Centuries, Volume 1: German Church Records

Bucks County, Pennsylvania, Church Records of the 17th and 18th Centuries, Volume 2: Quaker Records: Falls and Middletown Monthly Meetings
Anna Miller Watring and F. Edward Wright

Bucks County, Pennsylvania, Church Records of the 17th and 18th Centuries, Volume 4

Caroline County, Maryland, Marriages, Births and Deaths, 1850–1880

Citizens of the Eastern Shore of Maryland, 1659–1750

Colonial Families of Cape May County, New Jersey, Revised 2nd Edition

Colonial Families of Delaware:
Volumes: Volume 1; Volume 2: Kent and Sussex Counties; Volume 3 (2nd Edition): Kent and Sussex Counties; Volume 4: Sussex County; Volume 5: New Castle; Volume 6: Kent County

Lancaster County, Pennsylvania, Church Records of the 18th Century, Volume 5

Lancaster County, Pennsylvania, Church Records of the 18th Century: Volume 6
Robert L. Hess and F. Edward Wright

*Lancaster County, Virginia, Marriage References
and Family Relationships, 1650–1800*

Land Records of Sussex County, Delaware, 1769–1782

Land Records of Sussex County, Delaware, 1782–1789: Deed Book N No. 13
Elaine Hastings Mason and F. Edward Wright

Marriage Licenses of Washington, District of Columbia, 1811–1830

*Marriage References and Family Relationships of Charles City,
Prince George, and Dinwiddie Counties, Virginia, 1634–1800*

Marriages and Deaths from Eastern Shore Newspapers, 1790–1835

*Marriages and Deaths from the Newspapers of Allegany
and Washington Counties, Maryland, 1820–1830*

Marriages and Deaths from the York Recorder, *1821–1830*

*Marriages and Deaths in the Newspapers of Frederick
and Montgomery Counties, Maryland, 1820–1830*

*Marriages and Deaths in the Newspapers of
Lancaster County, Pennsylvania, 1821–1830*

*Marriages and Deaths in the Newspapers of
Lancaster County, Pennsylvania, 1831–1840*

Marriages and Deaths of Cumberland County, [Pennsylvania], 1821–1830

Marriages, Births, Deaths and Removals of New Castle County, Delaware

*Maryland Calendar of Wills:
Volume 9: 1744–1749; Volume 10: 1748–1753; Volume 11: 1753–1760;
Volume 12: 1759–1764; Volume 13: 1764–1767; Volume 14: 1767–1772;
Volume 15: 1772–1774; and Volume 16: 1774–1777*

*Maryland Eastern Shore Newspaper Abstracts
Volume 1: 1790–1805; Volume 2: 1806–1812;
Volume 3: 1813–1818; Volume 4: 1819–1824;
Volume 5: Northern Counties, 1825–1829*
F. Edward Wright and Irma Harper;
*Volume 6: Southern Counties, 1825–1829;
Volume 7: Northern Counties, 1830–1834*
Irma Harper and F. Edward Wright;
Volume 8: Southern Counties, 1830–1834

*Maryland Eastern Shore Vital Records:
Book 1: 1648–1725, Second Edition; Book 2: 1726–1750; Book 3: 1751–1775;
Book 4: 1776–1800; and Book 5: 1801–1825*

*Maryland Militia in the War of 1812:
Volume 1: Eastern Shore; Volume 2: Baltimore City and County;
Volume 3: Cecil and Harford Counties; Volume 4: Anne Arundel and Calvert Counties;
Volume 5: St. Mary's and Charles Counties; Volume 6: Prince George's County;
and Volume 7: Montgomery County*

Maryland Militia in the Revolutionary War
S. Eugene Clements and F. Edward Wright